Elizabeth Scott's book, *Raindrops on Roman*, has been an inspiration to thousands of parents and teachers who deal with children within the rainbow of markers associated with autism. Her fabulous book has created a demand for a "how to" manual to reach and teach children with these special needs. Her new book, the *Autism Recovery Manual*, co-authored with Lynne Gillis is a complete and practical guide enabling special students to make amazing developmental progress. The book is an extraordinary tool parents and educators can use to connect with children within the autism spectrum. It provides keys to unlock the learning potential of the child you yearn to help.

~ Tom Wilson, Ph.D., Public School Superintendent, Lancaster, Texas
Author of *A Chance At Life*

The *Autism Recovery Manual* is a fine handbook for parents looking for resources and activities to develop the minds and skills of children with autism. Scott and Gillis have documented and explained dozens and dozens of activities designed to help children progress through developmental stages to reach more mature levels of functioning. The book is structured into categories covering domains of development, such as motor skills, sensory skills, and critical thinking. The activities presented are very practical, and they underpin the brain hemispheric integration necessary for adaptive functioning. Parents of children with autism will find this book a useful guide for helping their children maximize their potential.

~ Mark Steinberg, Ph.D., Clinical Neuropsychologist
Coauthor with Siegried Othmer, Ph.D. of *ADD: The 20-Hour Solution: Attention Deficit Disorder and the Healing Effects of EEG Neurofeedback*

The *Autism Recovery Manual of Skills and Drills* is a fantastic useful resource to use in the classroom. The manual offers helpful information for all children that can easily be organized into centers and activities. The Skills and Drills are useful for children diagnosed with autism or any disability. Parents and families can read and find Drills they can incorporate into their everyday life. They can start the recovery process minutes after reading a Skill from the manual and put into action additional Skills and Drills day after day. I like that it offers many different therapy activities that are easy to understand. The pictures give realistic information that go along with the Skills and offers hope to all of us working with children today.

As a kindergarten teacher, I implemented the Skills and Drills into my centers the very next day after getting the manual. It offered me a different approach to activities with a purpose that went with my lesson plans. The Skills and Drills offer different activities that go with a students learning style. Gently introducing activities can help students overcome their fears and build self-esteem while learning. The activities will offer hope and purpose for children who are developmentally behind or need extra therapy during school hours in the LRE (Least Restrictive Environment). I will share the manual with the special education department at my school. It is especially helpful for inclusion coaches who work with regular classroom teachers that may not have a special education certification. The CRS plan shows the importance of not giving up and is aligned with a teacher's approach of consistency, praise, and re-teaching.

I do not want one child to go without the valuable information this manual has to offer. I look forward to hearing more success stories after parents and schools get their hands on this outstanding resource. Thank you Elizabeth and Roman for sharing truly valuable information that will benefit many children and their families!

~ Paige Garza, Kindergarten Teacher
Cockrell Hill Elementary, DeSoto, Texas (Roman's first preschool teacher)

The *Autism Recovery Manual of Skills and Drills* was created to help children with autism. This book teaches all of us how and why to play with our children. Play is the work of childhood. This book is an excellent resource for all parents and professionals to lead children through their developmental stages to reach their potential.

~ Norann Lafon, M.A., Special Education, Reading Decoding Specialist for forty-plus years and author of *The Seven Syllable Seminars* and *Reading Week Seminar*

As a longtime educator working with children of all abilities, I greatly respect the work that Elizabeth Burton Scott and Lynne Gillis have achieved in creating this *Autism Recovery Manual of Skills and Drills*. The book maps out the details of how to engage and stimulate any child's learning development. The curriculum is appropriate for all children and can provide the consistency, repetition, and structure that are the keys in Early Childhood Education.

The Skills and Drills introduce all the early developmental concepts for children in a thoughtful, interesting, and engaging manner. For all children, but specifically for children with early learning difficulties or attention disorders, these activities are purposeful and meaningful. Intensive daily use would certainly have a tremendous impact on a child's learning and his achievement of new developmental milestones.

~ Barry R. De St. Croix, M.A.
Former Executive Director of the Schwartz Center for Children, Dartmouth, MA
Over thirty-five years of professional experience working with children with special needs

Congratulations to Elizabeth Burton Scott and Lynne Gillis on their *Autism Recovery Manual of Skills and Drills* for parents, teachers and therapists. The activities are easy to use with materials that are readily available. Their attention to tasks that work to improve the child's focus, building transitions, and desensitizing skills and daily living activities are well done! This well organized approach will be beneficial to all those who strive to have children with autism reach their greatest potential.

~ Sandra A.B. Ledvina, M.S., Integrated Preschool/Special Education Teacher in a Public School System for thirty-two years

Skills and Drills is a positive, practical program that parents, teachers and therapists can use to enhance every child's development.

~ Johanna Duponte, Ed D, MS, OTR/L, Professor and Program Chair
Occupational Therapy Assistant Program, Bristol Community College

Elizabeth Scott's first book, *Raindrops on Roman*, is an inspiring story about how she helped her son overcome Autism. The manual includes the Skills and Drills that she developed to successfully facilitate teaching with Roman. As a former elementary educator, Elizabeth has broken down the Skills and Drills into multi-sensory, meaningful activities that can be incorporated throughout the day. I have implemented these Skills and Drills with my early elementary students, and they have demonstrated significant areas of improvement. Parents and teachers will finally have another tool that will help guide them to the path towards recovery.

~ Karen A. Oliveira, Special Educator and Graduate of Antioch University Autism Spectrum Disorders Certificate Program

The *Autism Recovery Manual of Skills and Drills* will be one of tremendous value to anyone who works with a special-needs child. It has provided me with an abundance of ideas and information that I will incorporate into my current intervention program. I have spent the past three years gathering information and materials in order to work more effectively with students who are in need of such a program. I wish I would have had this from day one. What a great resource! Thank you for sharing.

~ Ronda Johnson, Special Education

Autism Recovery Manual of Skills and Drills is very well organized and thought out. The activities for all phases of communication and motor organization are practical and easy to incorporate into any daily routine. The text feels like a well-worn manual of key ideas from a long-time educator/practitioner! Highly recommended. Congratulations on such a comprehensive project!

~ Suzanne Crouch, B.A., M.Ed.
Former Language-Based Teacher and Speech Pathologist

Autism Recovery Manual of Skills and Drills

A Preschool and Kindergarten Education Program for Parents, Teachers, and Therapists

By the Author of

Raindrops on Roman
Overcoming Autism: A Message of Hope

Elizabeth Burton Scott
Masters in Elementary Education

and

Lynne Gillis
Occupational Therapist

Robert D. Reed Publishers • Bandon, OR • www.rdrpublishers.com

Robert D. Reed Publishers
P.O. Box 1992
Bandon, OR 97411
Phone: 541-347-9882; Fax: -9883
E-mail: 4bobreed@msn.com
Website: www.rdrpublishers.com

Editor: Kate Rakini
Front Cover Photos:
1. Rainbow © Joker productions – dreamstime.com
2. Open antique wooded trunk © kmit – fotolia.com
3. Toys in chest from Google Images, from photos by Cleone L. Reed, and two books from Robert D. Reed Publishers – *Rocky the Lighthouse Makes a Difference* by Jeffrey Noel and *The Biggest and Brightest Light* by Marily Perlyn and Amanda Perlyn

Back cover photo: Roman © Lifetouch Portraits
Cover Designer: Cleone L. Reed
Book Designer: Debby Gwaltney

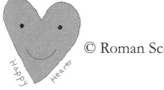 © Roman Scott

Mixed Sources
Product group from well-managed forests and other controlled sources
www.fsc.org Cert no. SW-COC-002283
© 1996 Forest Stewardship Council

ISBN 13: 978-1-934759-38-7
ISBN 10: 1-934759-38-4

Library of Congress Control Number: 2009936610

Manufactured, Typeset, and Printed in the United States of America

Dedication

To every parent, teacher, and therapist
who has helped a child
achieve his or her potential.

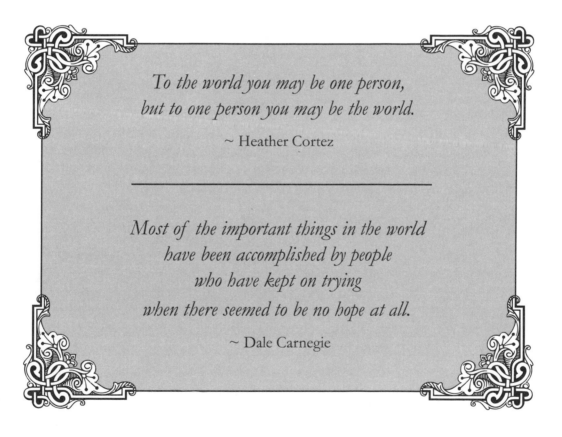

To the world you may be one person,
but to one person you may be the world.

~ Heather Cortez

Most of the important things in the world
have been accomplished by people
who have kept on trying
when there seemed to be no hope at all.

~ Dale Carnegie

ACKNOWLEDGMENTS

A special thank you to our publisher Robert Reed for his encouragement and support, and having the foresight to know that these Skills and Drills needed to be turned into a manual as an in-depth guideline for parents, teachers, and therapists to use. Thank you for another wonderful opportunity!

We want to acknowledge Cleone Reed
for her ingenious suggestions and creating another beautiful cover.

And Debby Gwaltney, a very talented graphics designer,
for designing a beautiful book.

To Kate Rakini for her guidance, review, and edits of our manuscript.

To Lila Hosbjor Hinchy, MS CCC SLP, Speech-Language Pathologist,
for her contributions and professional expertise.

We wish to thank our husbands for their patience, understanding, and support.
We want to express our gratitude to Roman Scott for being
so socially gracious and a wonderful media guest and book promoter.
He is the reason the Skills and Drills program was created, and he is a shining
example of just how much can be done for children with autism.

TABLE OF CONTENTS

PART ONE: LANGUAGE SKILLS

PART TWO: SENSORY SKILLS

PART THREE: FINE MOTOR SKILLS

PART FOUR: GROSS MOTOR SKILLS

PART FIVE: CONCEPT SKILLS

PART SIX: SELF- CARE/ACTIVITIES OF DAILY LIVING

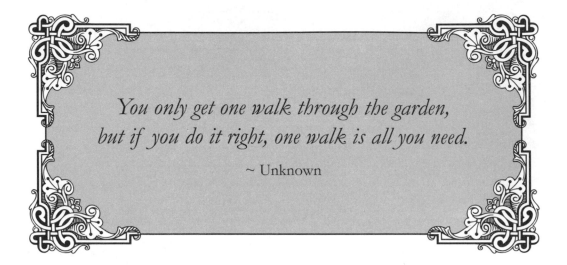

You only get one walk through the garden,
but if you do it right, one walk is all you need.

~ Unknown

PREFACE

My son Roman was diagnosed with autism at 18 months. He had a total of 45 symptoms that he needed to overcome. Roman could not talk, could not eat, engaged in repetitive behaviors, fixated on objects, and had a myriad of sensory, fine, and gross motor problems. He began Early Childhood Intervention at 18 months of age. His intervention included one-hour sessions of speech and occupational therapy three days a week. I attended each session with Roman and applied the techniques the therapists taught me and developed my own in-home therapy program I call "Skills and Drills," published in my book *Raindrops on Roman*, the story of his recovery from autism.

The purpose of the Skills and Drills program was to help Roman overcome his autistic behaviors through learning activities and meaningful play. Each Skill and Drill was designed to achieve a specific goal. Everything that Roman was afraid to do or could not do, I had to encourage and teach him to do. As a former elementary teacher, I used my teaching and classroom techniques and applied them to Roman. The Skills and Drills I used were multi-sensory tasks to develop and stimulate every part of his brain and all of his senses, which I believe was critical for his recovery.

The Skills and Drills program is an intensive intervention program that involves working with a child on a daily basis. I worked with Roman up to ten hours a day for nearly three years, and I incorporated these Skills into his activities of daily living, such as feeding, dressing, bathing, riding in the car, and bedtime routines. I tried to engage my son in purposeful learning activities or meaningful play throughout the day.

The *Autism Recovery Manual* contains 90 Skills and Drills including all of the original 78 Skills and Drills that were used to accomplish Roman's full recovery from autism. On his fourth birthday he no longer tested with symptoms on the autism spectrum and no longer needed any special education or a therapy program. Today, Roman is enrolled in a traditional second grade class and excels in academics and sports, and is able to relate socially to adults and his peers.

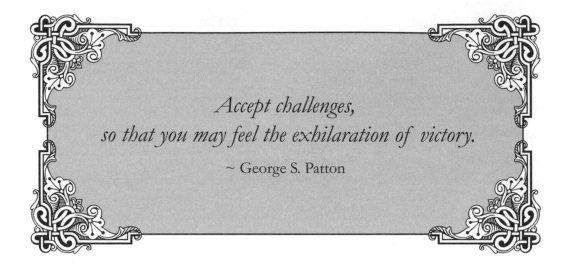

Accept challenges,
so that you may feel the exhilaration of victory.

~ George S. Patton

INTRODUCTION

The Autism Recovery Manual of Skills and Drills was written for parents, teachers, and therapists because the recovery that Roman experienced needed to be shared. Skills and Drills is a preschool and kindergarten education program that helps to develop the whole child. A child with autism benefits from being involved in a learning activity or meaningful play that keeps the child's mind focused to keep the child from engaging in repetitive or negative behaviors or retreating into his own world. The Skills and Drills Program includes activities that encourage development in language, sensory motor, fine motor, gross motor, concept skills, self-care, and activities for daily living. Each Skill and Drill is divided into four parts: Explanation of the Skill, Develops and Improves, Suggested Dialogue, and Additional Activities. The original 78 Skills and Drills have been enhanced and expanded upon, along with many new activities to encourage a child's development.

BENEFITS OF SKILLS AND DRILLS:

- This manual includes easy-to-understand and simple-to-follow suggestions for meaningful fun activities that promote a young child's development.

- Teaching children between the ages of one and five is extremely beneficial because a child's brain is so amenable to learning.

- Mastering these Skills will enable a child to be confident and excited about learning and will ease many frustrations or anxieties.

- Parents, therapists, and teachers can select which Skills and Drills best fit the child's developmental needs.

- The program is designed to promote a child's cognitive development and learning capabilities through meaningful activities while providing the child with a desire to learn.

- Every child will benefit from an early learning program of consistency, repetition, and structure.

- There are minimal costs for the toys and supplies needed for Skills and Drills, which can be purchased at local stores in your community.

Overview

The following is a list of the techniques and approaches the parent, teacher, or therapist should implement in order to execute an effective Skills and Drills program. Every child's needs are different, but these guidelines apply to all children regardless of their particular challenges.

Set Up:

Set up a well-organized program that will run smoothly and effectively. Gather all of the materials you are going to use and store all the supplies in labeled containers, toy chests, or on shelves in a designated area of your classroom, home, or clinic. This organization will facilitate locating the necessary supplies and will ease the transition from one activity to the next. Have a recognized "clean-up" time and assist the child in putting away any supplies or toys used. It is important to teach the child to clean up and put things away after each activity.

CRS Plan:

Parents need to be committed to a CRS plan: *Consistency, Repetition, and Structure. Consistency* is working with the child everyday. The Skills and Drills need to be *repeated* over and over again until each Skill is mastered. It is suggested that the activities be done in a *structured* and familiar environment, such as the home or preschool setting.

MEEP Approach:

It is important to use this four-step approach with each Skill: 1) *Model,* 2) *Engage,* 3) *Encourage,* and 4) *Praise. Model* the activity you want the child to do. Help him *engage* in the activity. *Encourage* him while doing the activity, and give lots of *praise* and cheers once the activity is completed.

Practical Time Frames:

Parents, teachers, or therapists should work with the child with autism as often as their schedule permits. The more time spent on meaningful and structured activities and play, the greater the improvement. Also, the Skills and Drills can be used with any preschool or kindergarten child. Doing 20-30 minutes several times a week, learning and mastering the Skills and Drills, will help prepare your child for kindergarten.

Schedule/Rewards:

It may be a good idea to have an organized daily schedule of Skills and Drills for the child. Make a list of the daily activities and alternate between fine motor, gross motor, sensory motor, and language skills. A schedule will allow the teacher, therapist, or parent to see all the activities they will be doing or have done for the day and through the week. This will provide encouragement and keep you organized by outlining the activities of the day. Check off completed Skills and Drills.

Have a wish list of activities that the child can choose to do each day. You may want to make pictures of the various activities for the child to view so he will know which Skills he will be doing or what he has done for the day. You should also implement a task related reward system for the child's accomplishments. Choose rewards that will motivate each child such as, stickers, stamps, story time, play time with a specific toy, or healthy snack.

Transitions:
It is important to have a transition time when going from one activity to another in order to ease a child's anxieties or frustrations about ending an activity. The parent, teacher, or therapist should have countdowns and say, for example, "Two more minutes, then it is time to clean up. One more minute, 30 seconds…" Then count from one to ten. This way the child will have time to process that the activity is almost over and lessen any frustration. Do this with all the Skills and Drills if the child has a difficult time transitioning.

Table Time/Floor Time:
Be sure to alternate from table-time to floor-time activities so the child will not be sitting too long in one place. It is important that you are down on the floor at eye level with the child because you are giving the child visual cues and teaching attention to task during floor time activities and imaginative floor play.

Encourage Eye-Contact:
If the child avoids eye contact, encourage the child to look at you when you talk to him and when he talks to you. It is important to work on establishing eye contact with him. For example, say to the child, "Look at me," or "Look at my eyes," while physically motioning with two fingers in a "V" position moving toward your eyes. This will cue the child where to look. Try to establish eye contact before and during each Skill and Drill. If the child refuses to look at you, be sure to move your face in front of his so he can see you while you talk to him. If the child looks away when he responds, gently move his chin in the direction of your face to establish some eye contact.

Focusing Ability:
It is so important that the child learns how to focus and attend. Without the ability to focus and attend, one cannot easily concentrate, and therefore remember or recall. If the child is not able to stay focused, try using a kitchen timer for each Skill to increase

his attention span. The timer should be set for the time interval you believe the child can handle for each Skill. Begin at his attention ability. For example, if he can focus for two minutes, set the timer for two minutes, and then increase to three, four, or five minutes as his attention span increases. Have the child sit and engage in a particular Skill until the timer goes off. Do not allow him to get up from the activity until the timer goes off. If the child needs a time-out during the activity, then place him in a time-out chair, and then redirect him back to the same activity.

Stimming:

Many children with autism do something called stimming. This self-stimulatory behavior reduces sensory overload and/or can stimulate a child's senses. The child may engage in repetitive body movements involving any of the five senses, including behaviors such as staring or fixating on objects like ceiling fans and lights, opening and closing fists, moving fingers in front of his face, hand flapping, or waving, lining up objects, running around in circles, rocking back and forth, shrieking or yelling out, or echolalia. When a child begins to stim, transition him using countdowns from the stimming activity and replace the behavior with something positive, such as a toy, or begin clapping or singing to distract or redirect him to a positive activity.

Hand Over Hand Assistance:

If the child is unable or unwilling to perform a task, gently place your hand over his to guide him through the task until he feels comfortable or is able to obtain success. Say to the child, "Let's do it together." This will help ease or lessen his anxiety so that you can then teach him how to perform the specific task.

Overcoming Fears:

If the child is afraid of certain sounds, objects, activities, try to help him overcome each fear. The teachers, therapists, or parent should encourage and teach the child anything that he is afraid to or cannot do. For example, if the child is afraid of a specific instrument sound, gently introduce and expose the child to the instrument, and softly play the sound. Repeat this drill daily until he is no longer fearful of the noise. Do this with all tactile (touch) substances he may be afraid to touch, such as finger paint, glue, and feathers. Introduce items gently and slowly reassuring the child that he has nothing to fear. Make up or sing a song about the object he fears.

Self-Care/Activities of Daily Living (ADL):

Parents can incorporate many of the Skills and Drills into the activities of daily living, such as dressing, mealtime, bath time, riding in the car, and bedtime routines.

The child can be engaged in learning activity or meaningful play while the parent is doing household chores. For example, while the parent is making dinner, or during meal time, be sure to have a "goody bag of toys" for the child to play with to keep him engaged and focused. These can include board books, puzzles, stacking cups, alphabet letters or numbers, or shape sorter. (See Appendix I for "goody bag of toys for mealtime.") Be prepared to interchange these toys, so when the child is finished playing with one toy you can quickly give him another.

Conclusion

The purpose of the Skills and Drills program is to teach children how to sit, focus, follow directions, learn, and master a variety of basic developmental skills and engage in learning activity and meaningful play in a structured environment. These skills and techniques apply to all preschool children, whether they are a typical child with or without an accompanying diagnosis of ADD, ADHD, sensory processing disorder, or autism.

For the child with autism, getting a child to master many of these skills will be a giant step towards significant improvement. A one-to-one intensive early intervention program will be beneficial to the child's developmental progress. Many children may not improve quickly or obtain full recovery, but if you take the time to work with a child on a daily basis, using a consistent, repetitive, and structured program such as Skills and Drills, a child may achieve his fullest potential. We believe this is success!

PART ONE

Language Skills

"All language verbal, nonverbal, and written requires the most complex integration of sensory and motor information. It is an abstraction of personal experiences, and the ability to share and relate to experiences is essential in developing relationships with others."*

In order to build language skills, you need to immerse the child in language. Therefore, use lots of language when doing *all* the Skills and Drills. The manual provides suggested dialogues to use for each activity in order to encourage the child to talk. If the child can speak, ask questions and model answers in complete three- or four-word sentences. Praise his response, short or long, and continue to model. Then increase to five- to eight-word sentences, and so on. If he is unable to answer or does not answer appropriately, give him the language by modeling the appropriate response and encourage him to repeat it. Use the same consistent words. This will build vocabulary, articulation ability, and correct sentence structure. It will also enable the child to verbalize his feelings, thus increase his ability to engage in conversation, share experiences, and relate to others.

Be sure to engage in a great deal of language and dialogue in each of the Skills and Drills throughout the day. Language exercises and drills will increase social skills because the child will be able to interact more appropriately with his peers and family during a variety of activities and events.

It is important to realize that if the child has significantly delayed receptive language, he will not be able to perform many of these tasks. The expectations will need to be adjusted for this child. Such tasks should be attempted; however, it is important to adjust your individual objectives for each child so that he can feel that he has indeed achieved some level of success with each attempt. For example, for a child with low levels of receptive language skills, you will need to teach vocabulary by labeling objects. Show the child items in the house or school, and have him hold each one while you say the word. Take his finger and point to the object, "Ball." Later, you will say, "Point to the ball." Next, you will provide him a choice of two familiar objects (one being the ball) and say, "Point to the ball." If you cannot establish a point, simply ask the child to show you the ball. If he can indicate to you with his eyes that he is choosing the ball, that is a successful *first* step. Remember, the objective for each child will be different.

* Maryann Colby Trott, M.A., Marci K. Laurel, M.A., CCC-SLP, and Susan L. Windeck, M.S., OTR/L. *SenseAbilities: Understanding Sensory Integration.* (USA: The Psychological Corporation, 1993), p. 1.

18

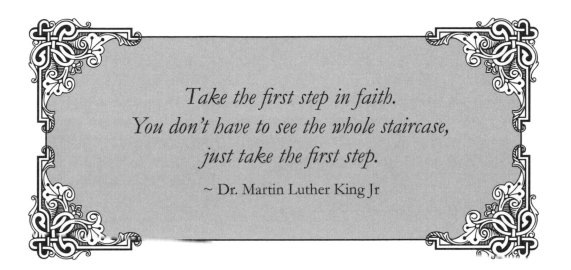

Take the first step in faith.
You don't have to see the whole staircase,
just take the first step.

~ Dr. Martin Luther King Jr

1. Reading

Read a variety of books that teach about things in the child's world, such as shapes, colors, animals, numbers, nature, farm, school, transportation, and the park. Have the child sit, facing you, on the floor and read him a book. This will prepare him for listening  experiences in the classroom. Point to various pictures and encourage him to identify what is in the picture. If he is not yet talking, name items in the pictures in the book and have him point to them. If he is speaking, make up short sentences and have him repeat them. If he is hesitant to repeat, try starting the sentence for him and having him finish (sentence closure). It is important that he learns how to sit and focus during story time. Read two or more books to him everyday.

Develops/Improves: Language, vocabulary, memory, concentration, and attention span.

Suggested Dialogue: Engage the child in conversation after reading a book about going to the park. Ask the child, "Do you like to go to the park?" If the child does not respond, model the answer by saying, "I like to go to the park," and encourage the child to repeat the answer. Ask the child additional questions, such as, "What is your favorite thing to do in the park?" Again, model the answer for the child by saying, "I like to swing." Encourage lots of language by reading books.

Additional Activities:

- Read to the pictures on the page in a predictable fashion. Feel free to make up your own words for each page to hold the child's attention. Keep the sentences short (three to six words) using consistency and repetition. For example: "The cat says meow." "The cow lives on a farm." "The car is red."

- Read books about their favorite television shows or videos, such as *Baby Einstein, Little Bear, Handy Mandy, Dora, The Mickey Mouse Club, Max and Ruby, Barney, Calliou,* and *Thomas and Friends.*

- Visit the library during the major holidays, such as Valentine's Day, Easter, Halloween, Thanksgiving, Chanukah, and Christmas. Take home a picture book about each holiday to read to the child. Enjoy this special time together.

- Listen to the *Look, Read, and Listen* books while traveling in a car.

2. Touch and Feel Books

Read an assortment of textured books. Have the child touch and feel the variety of surfaces and textures in the books. Name the different textures, such as soft, wooly, hairy, bumpy, furry, spongy, shiny, rough, and smooth. Have him say the word associated with different pictures and textures in the book.

Develops/Improves: Language, vocabulary, sensory awareness, and discrimination skills.

Suggested Dialogue: Ask the child to point to the bunny. Respond, "Good job, nice pointing." Then ask the child, "How does the bunny feel?" Model the answer for the child if he does not respond by saying, "The bunny feels soft." Ask the child, "How does the sand feel?" Encourage the child to reply, "The sand feels rough."

If the child responds with "Rough." Then praise the child, "Great!" and continue with, "That's right, the sand is rough." You have built your model sentence into your praise sentence.

Additional Activities:

- To reinforce language while reading touch and feel books, give the child a three- or four-word sentence to say about each picture, such as, "The bunny is soft." If he is able to talk, have him repeat it.

- *Touch and Feel Picture Cards*: Hands-On-Learning by Scholastic or DK Publishing has four sets of *Touch and Feel Picture Cards* of animals, numbers, colors and shapes, and first words.

- Show him an object in the room that is soft, such as a blanket or a stuffed animal. Ask him to bring you something soft.

- Place a piece of contact paper with sticky side up and have the child put feathers, cotton balls, and various other small pieces of textured items on the sticky side of the paper to create a "touch and feel" collage. Encourage the child to tell how each item feels to touch.

3. Word Chart

Make a word chart of all the words he learns how to say. Have the child repeat all the words each day in order for him to learn and remember how to say them. Add to the word chart with each new word he says. This will be exciting and encouraging for you and him.

Word Chart

ball	blue
cat	no
mama	book
more	toy
go	block
door	sun
dog	water
car	baby
doll	tub
truck	me

Develops/Improves: Language, memory, and auditory processing skills.

Suggested Dialogue: Use the child's name with words he knows how to say, such as, "This is Paul's cup," and "Paul plays with the ball."

Additional Activities:

- Make a picture chart of all the words the child can say and have him name the word for each picture.

- Point to pictures in a book related to words he can say.

- Make a picture book of words he can say. Encourage him to point to and name each object.

- Say words that rhyme with the words the child can say.

4. Nursery Song Sing Along

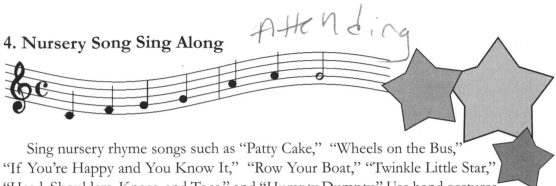

Attending

Sing nursery rhyme songs such as "Patty Cake," "Wheels on the Bus," "If You're Happy and You Know It," "Row Your Boat," "Twinkle Little Star," "Head, Shoulders, Knees, and Toes," and "Humpty Dumpty." Use hand gestures while singing and provide hand-over-hand assistance with gestures as needed. Have him play musical instruments while you sing together.

Develops/Improves: Language, vocabulary, rhyming words, fine motor skills, manual dexterity, and eye-hand coordination skills.

Suggested Dialogue: Tell the child it is "song time," and name each song before singing it. Sing the same two or three songs each day while mixing up additional songs for variety. Praise the child for his good listening skills saying, "Nice clapping" or "Nice singing." Try asking the child what song he would like to sing together with you. Give him a choice of two songs.

Additional Activities:

- Listen to nursery rhyme CDs while traveling in the car.

- For the words to the nursery rhyme songs, go to www.google.com and type in nursery rhymes.

- Read and listen to the **Fisher Price Story Book Rhymes** electronic toy.

5. Shape Sorter

Place different shapes in front the child and have him say the various shapes by name and place the shapes into the correct slots. If he is not yet talking, say the name of a shape and have him pick it up and place it in the matching slot.

Develops/Improves: Language, shape discrimination and recognition, fine motor skills, eye-hand coordination, and spatial relations skills.

Suggested Dialogue: Encourage lots of dialogue while playing. Ask the child, "What shape is this?" "What color is the square?" and "Is the ball shaped like a circle or a square?"

Additional Activities:

- Circle, square, triangle **Large Knob Puzzle** by Melissa and Doug.

- DK Publishing *Shapes*, *Color,* and *Touch and Feel* picture cards.

- Play "Shapes Bingo."

- Play "Shapes Dominoes."

6. Learning Shapes

Get a three-piece puzzle containing a circle, square, and triangle. Name the shapes. Have the child point to and pick up the shape and place it into the puzzle. Have him say the name of each shape. Once mastered, teach more shapes with an eight-piece puzzle.

Develops/Improves: Shape discrimination and recognition, fine motor skills, eye-hand coordination, and spatial relations skills.

Suggested Dialogue: Ask the child, "What shape is round?" "What shape has three sides?" "What shape has four sides?" and "What shape is a ball?"

Additional Activities:

- Play "Mix and Pick." Mix up the shapes on a table. Name a shape and have the child find it.

- **House Jumbo Knob Puzzle** (**First Shapes** by Melissa and Doug): Teaches triangle, circle, oval, rectangle, and square shapes on a house. Have him name the different color of each shape and place it on the house puzzle. Advance to the **8-Piece Shapes Jumbo Puzzle** (by Melissa and Doug).

- Give the child a circle and have him point to or name something in the room that is a circle, i.e., toy ball, hula-hoop, or a round clock on the wall. Repeat this game for all shapes. Find something square (jack-in the box), triangular (triangle instrument), and rectangular (dining room table).

- Play **Candy Land Castle** game: color match and sort shapes.

7. Learning Colors

Using a poster of different colored balloons, shapes, or any fun objects showing colors, teach the child to name all the colors. Point to each one and name the color. Have him point to it. Then go on to the next color. Teach one color each day or week, depending on how quickly he learns. Have him pronounce the word for each color. If he is not yet talking, encourage him to say the initial consonant sound like "b" for blue, and have him point to it. Go over the colors he has already learned to ensure that he remembers them. Then go on to the next color. Complete all primary colors. Keep going over the colors with him each day.

Develops/Improves: Language, thinking, and color recognition skills.

Suggested Dialogue: Point to the blue balloon and say, "This is the blue balloon." Then ask, "Which one is the blue balloon?" Repeat for all colors.

Additional Activities:

- Go on a nature walk through the park and name all the different colored objects you see (trees, grass, sky, bird). Then ask, "What color is the sky?" Encourage the child to reply, "The sky is blue."

- Using colored counters or blocks, have your child name the color and sort the items by color into a container.

- Give the child a red block and have him name something in the room that is red, i.e., his red shirt or a red toy car.

- Tower blocks of matching colors.

- Play the **Candy Land** game.

- Play the **Twister** game.

8. Puzzles

Use a variety of floor and table puzzles to teach about all the different places, objects, and things he needs to know about in his world, such as shapes, alphabet, numbers, transportation, sports, fruits and vegetables, types of animals (pets, farm, zoo, and ocean animals). Encourage your child to talk about and point to different puzzle pieces, then have him place them in the correct spot.

Develops/Improves: Language, vocabulary, fine motor skills, eye-hand coordination, and spatial relations skills

Suggested Dialogue: Point to a puzzle piece and ask the child, "What is this a picture of?" Respond by saying, "This is a car." Then ask, "What color is the car?" Reply by saying, "This is a red car."

Additional Activities:

- Mix and Play: Say the name of different puzzle pieces for him to find.

- Make a simple three- or four-piece puzzle by cutting a picture of a favorite toy from a magazine or photo.

9. Play Animals

Get sets of farm, wild, and pet animals. Teach the child the names of the animals and the sounds they make. Categorize them into farm, wild, and pet animals. Have him hold the animals and move them around. Play "Find the Animal." Let him watch as you hide an animal behind a toy or under a pillow and ask, "Where did the tiger go?" Have him find it and try to say the animal's name. Show him the dog and say, "Dog. The dog says, 'Woof-woof.'" Line up a few animals and have him point to the different animals and say their sounds.

Develops/Improves: Language, vocabulary, articulation, and auditory creativity, memory, and imagination skills.

Suggested Dialogue: Ask the child what sound the animal makes. Then say "Meow" and have him guess which animal you are imitating. Encourage the child to tell you where the animal lives.

Additional Activities:

- Have the child set up a zoo with play animals and pretend to visit the zoo. Encourage the child to tell you about each animal.

- Take the child to a zoo and talk about each animal.

- Go to a pond to feed the ducks and facilitate the use of language: "The ducks like to eat bread. The ducks swim in the water. How many ducks do you see? What should we feed the ducks?"

10. Farm Play

Using a play farm kit encourage the child to use imaginative play with the animals, a barn, and other things you would find on a farm. Teach him to say the names of the animals and their sounds.

Develops/Improves: Language, vocabulary, articulation, auditory memory, creativity, and imagination.

Suggested Dialogue: Ask the child, "What does a lamb say?" and "What color is a lamb?" Encourage the child to tell you how it feels to touch a lamb.

Additional Activities:

- Go to the library and find a book about farm animals. Encourage dialogue about each animal pictured in the book.

- Visit a real farm or petting zoo to see the animals.

- Sing animal songs together, such as "Old MacDonald Had a Farm."

- Read *Touch and Feel* animal books together.

11. Circus Play

Using a play circus kit encourage the child to use imaginative play with the animals, clowns, a tent, and other apparatus you would find at a circus. Have the child name the different animals and objects in the circus.

Develops/Improves: Language, vocabulary, articulation, creativity, and imagination.

Suggested Dialogue: Have the child name the different animals and objects in the circus. Have him say sentences about different objects and people in the circus. If the child is not yet talking, say the name of an object and have him point to it.

Additional Activities:

- Go to the library and find a book about the circus. Encourage a great deal of dialogue about each picture in the book.

- Take the child to the circus. Immerse him in an abundance of dialogue.

12. Puppets

Use puppets representing things from everyday life, such as animals, family, and career puppets, i.e., doctor, nurse, policeman, or construction worker. Place puppets on the child's hands and act out events.

Develops/Improves: Language, storytelling, role-playing, imagination, and socialization skills.

Suggested Dialogue: Engage in conversation about each puppet. Ask the child, "What animal is the puppet?" Provide a response for the child to repeat, such as, "The puppet is a lion." Also, for career puppets, ask the child questions, such as, "Who helps you across the street?" and "Who do you go to when you are sick?"

Additional Activities:

- Go to a puppet show at the library.

- Put on a puppet show with the child choosing his favorite puppet for the performance. Use the kitchen or coffee table for the stage. Introduce the puppets and puppeteers. Have family members be the audience and give lots of applause at the end of the performance.

13. Telephone Talk

Pretend to call the child on a play cell phone and teach him to talk into the phone. Ask the child a variety of easy age-appropriate questions for him to answer. When he is not sure, model the response for him. This helps him to learn how to talk on the phone as well as talk how to communicate in complete three- to four-word sentences.

Develops/Improves: Language and socialization skills.

Suggested Dialogue: Hold the pretend phone and say to the child, "Who is this?" Encourage the child to reply, "This is (child's name)." Then ask, "How are you today?" Model the response, "I am fine," if needed.

Additional Activities:

- Call a family member or a friend on a real phone to practice social skills.

- Encourage social skills by having the child engage in everyday conversation that would be appropriate for his age group. Ask questions and have the child answer in complete sentences. If he doesn't know what to say or how to express it, tell him exactly what to say. If he doesn't say it, say it again for him to hear the appropriate response. Repeat these conversations daily.

- Play with child walkie-talkies.

14. Number Drills

Use a set of numbers one through nine. Begin with number one. Say to the child, "This is the number 'one'. Can you say 'one'?" Point to the number and encourage him to repeat it. Then have him point to the number and try to say it. Have him hold the number. Keep a list of each number he says. Introduce one number each day or week, depending on how fast he learns. Make sure he learns that number before you go on to the next. If he cannot say it, have him point to it. Review all the numbers he has learned each day. Use a numbers puzzle. Have him identify each number and place it in the puzzle. Encourage the child to point to and name numbers in a number book.

Develops/Improves: Language; number matching, selection and recognition; eye-hand coordination; spatial relations skills.

Suggested Dialogue: Ask the child to point to the number "one." Respond by saying to the child, "Good job! Nice pointing." Repeat for each number, one through nine. Ask the child, "How many hands do you have?" Reply to the child, "You have two hands."

Additional Activities:

- Play "Mix and Pick." Once the child has learned his numbers, mix them up on a table and have him find the number that you request. "Where is the number 'four'?" Encourage the child to reply, "Here is the number 'four'."

- Use Melissa and Doug's small grasp peg number puzzle.

- Use DK Publishing's *My First Numbers* and *Counting, Touch,* and *Feel* picture cards to practice number identification play.

- Sing "Five Little Monkeys" and use a finger counting demonstration while singing song together.

- Play with a large, foam number floor puzzle. Start with numbers one to three only. Gradually add other numbers as the child's ability develops.

- Count the number of stairs as you climb up and down a stairway.

15. Teddy Bear Counters

Practice counting, sorting, and patterning colored teddy bears. Have the child count teddy bears from one to ten.

Develops/Improves: Visual perception, language, color recognition, and counting skills.

Suggested Dialogue: Encourage the child to count the teddy bears and name the different colors.

Additional Activities:

- Play simple "color matching bingo" using colored teddy bears to fill up a card to win.

16. Alphabet Drills

Use a set of upper-case alphabet letters. Begin with the letter "A." Say to the child, "This is the letter 'A.' Can you say 'A'?" Point to the letter and encourage the child to repeat it. Then have him point to the letter and try to say it. Have him hold the letter. Give him that letter for the day. That will be his letter buddy. Do the alphabet in order. Introduce one letter each day or week, depending on how fast he learns. Keep a list of each letter he is able to say. Make sure he learns that letter before you go on to the next. If he cannot say it, have the child point to it (as in "show me the letter __" in a group of two). Review all the letters he has learned each day. Use a letters puzzle. Have him identify each letter and place them into the puzzle. Then encourage him to point to and name letters in an alphabet book.

Develops/Improves: Language; letter matching, letter selection, letter recognition; eye-hand coordination; spatial relations skills.

Suggested Dialogue: Ask the child to point to the letter "A." Respond by saying to the child, "Good job! Nice pointing." Then ask the child to name the letter. Again, respond by saying, "Good job." Repeat for all 26 letters until mastered.

Additional Activities:

- Play "Mix and Pick." Once the child has learned some of the alphabet, mix up the letters that he knows on a table and ask him to find the letter that you say. "Where is the letter 'C'?" Encourage the child to reply, "Here is the letter 'C'." The more letters that he learns, the more you can add to the game.

- **Fridge Phonics:** A magnetic alphabet toy that can be placed on the refrigerator. When you place a letter in the slot, it will say the letter and its sound.

- Read the *Baby Einstein: Alphabooks* set which includes all 26 letters in small individual books with pictures of objects beginning with each letter.

- Sing the alphabet song to the child.

- Stack one-inch alphabet blocks and name each letter.

- Play with large, foam floor alphabet puzzles. Start by using only two or three letters at a time.

- Play memory games using letters. Start with only five letters to match.

- Make a sign with the child's name for his bedroom door. Point to and say the letters in the child's name to him each day.

35

17. Flash Cards

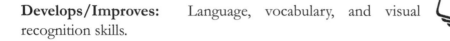

Use an assortment of flash cards of everyday objects, nature, animals, transportation, shapes, numbers, letters, food, and parts of the body. Have the child try to name the word associated with the picture on the flashcard.

Develops/Improves: Language, vocabulary, and visual recognition skills.

Suggested Dialogue: Ask the child, "What is this?" Reply, "This is a…."

Additional Activities:

- If the child is not yet talking, name what the picture is and have him point to it. If he is talking, have him try to make a sentence about each picture, or repeat a simple sentence, i.e., "The cat says 'Meow,'" or "I play with the ball."

- Association flashcards: Have him determine which objects in the picture belong together, i.e., bat/ball, paint brush/paint. If he is unable to explain, tell him the answer and have him repeat it. Ask the child, "What goes with the bat? The ball goes with the bat."

- Opposite cards: Teach him the concept of opposites: in/out, up/down, hot/cold. You can ask questions like, "What is the opposite of up? The opposite of up is down."

18. Activity Picture Cards

Show pictures of children's everyday routines, activities, and play, such as a child playing on the computer, playing baseball, playing soccer, eating, dressing, swinging, taking a bath, or sleeping. Have him describe what the child is doing in the picture in complete sentences.

Develops/Improves: Language, thinking, and pronoun usage.

Suggested Dialogue: Say to the child, "What is the boy doing?" Model a reply if the child does not answer. "He is eating lunch." If this is too difficult for the child, begin with the lower expectation of "He is eating." Encourage the child to build upon all responses if appropriate, while praising.

Additional Activities:

- Place several cards in front of him. Ask a question about one of the cards and have him point to the correct card. For example: "What card shows someone eating?" or "What card shows someone on a swing?"

- Emotional flash cards: Show pictures of a variety of children's expressions (happy, sad, mad, and scared). Teach the child to understand different facial expressions. This helps him to talk about his feelings and builds awareness of how he or others may feel. You can ask, "Do you think she is happy or sad?" You should make the same emotional face that is on the card and explain that emotion. Give an example of when one might feel that emotion.

19. Classifying Cards

Sort cards into groups of three things that go together. Classify cards into specific groups, such as toys, vehicles, shapes, animals, or foods. Have the child say words associated with the pictures in each group of cards.

Develops/Improves: Language, vocabulary, classification skills, thinking, and visual perception skills.

Suggested Dialogue: Have two piles of cards, one with toys and one with animals. Give the child the card with the picture of the dog. Ask, "What animal is this?" Model a response as needed, "This is a dog." Ask the child to place the dog in the animal pile. Respond by saying, "Nice job! The dog is an animal; it goes in the animal pile."

Additional Activities:

- Use four, five and six classifying cards as he masters the skill.

- Place cards in the wrong group and see if he can place them in the correct group.

- Facilitate the use of language by asking the child to label each object and to explain its function. Then, conclude by asking him which object is his favorite.

20. Felt Tales Storyboards

Create imaginative tales and different adventures with this 20-piece felt storyboard. Identify and reposition different objects to tell your own stories.

Develops/Improves: Language, eye-hand coordination, mental flexibility, and imagination.

Suggested Dialogue: Ask the child what animals are at the zoo or on the farm. Pretend you are one of the animals and go on a wonderful adventure with him at the farm or zoo.

Additional Activities:

- Play with a variety of felt storyboards, such as **Felt Tales Busy Day on the Farm Storyboard, Felt Tales Busy Day at the Zoo Storyboard, Felt Tales Noah's Ark Storyboard,** and **Felt Tales Happy Birthday Storyboard.** (See www.sensoryinterventions.com; under tactile toys)

21. Social Skills

Encourage the child to engage in everyday conversation that would be appropriate for his age group. Ask questions and have the child answer in complete sentences. If he does not know what to say or how to express it, tell him exactly what to say and have him repeat it. If he does not say it, say it again for him to hear the appropriate response. Repeat these conversations daily.

Develops/Improves: Language and socialization skills

Suggested Dialogue: Write down a list of questions and answers for the child to answer. Go over the same questions each day. For example, "What is your name? How old are you? What is your favorite color? What is your favorite toy? What do you like to eat? What is your favorite animal? What do you want to do today?" If the child does not answer, give the response and try to have him repeat it. If he cannot say it, then you say the correct response for him to hear.

Additional Activities:

- Practice social skills using toy cell phones.

- Call a family member or a friend on a real phone to practice social skills.

- Role-play for him the appropriate question-answer response at his age-level with two people so that he can watch and listen. One person will act as the child, himself, and the other as the person he is interacting with. This can also be done with two children who have been cued ahead of time.

22. Picnic in the Park

Pack a picnic basket with all his favorite foods, a blanket, even a portable CD player, and have a relaxing picnic in the park. Sit under a big tree or next to some flowers and let him enjoy the outdoors with you.

Develops/Improves: Language and socialization skills.

Suggested Dialogue: Ask the child to tell you what food items he would like to have in the picnic basket. Have the child help pack the picnic basket and name each item as he places it inside the basket.

Additional Activities:

- Read a book that shows a child on a picnic.

- Have a play date with a picnic in the park.

- During dinnertime at home, ask the child to tell you what he ate and what he liked best on the picnic.

23. Day Trips

Take a day trip to the zoo, a museum, a play, a bowling alley, a nature walk, or a farm.

Develops/Improves: Language and socialization skills.

Suggested Dialogue: Ask him questions about the different things he sees at each place. "What animals did you see today?" "What animal did you like best?" or "What was the tallest animal?"

Additional Activities:

- Read a book about the zoo before you go so the child will know what to expect and what he may be seeing. Have him name the different animals that are in the book. This will build excitement about going to the zoo.

- Play with the animal zoo kit and act out your trip to the zoo.

PART TWO

Sensory Skills

Sensory experiences include touch, movement, body awareness, sight, sound, and the pull of gravity. The process of organizing and interpreting this information is called sensory integration. Sensory integration provides a crucial foundation for later, more complex learning and behavior.

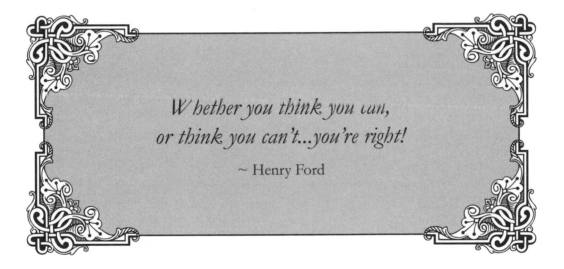

Whether you think you can,
or think you can't...you're right!

~ Henry Ford

24. Play Dough

Use a play dough kit that includes styling tools, such as shape cutters, rolling pin, EZ squeeze dough machine, stencils, and scissors. Have the child roll, squeeze, push, pull, poke, and cut play dough. Use a variety of shape cutters to cut out shapes, numbers, letters, and animals. Press small objects such as rocks, shells, and coins into the play dough.

Develops/Improves: Fine motor skills, dexterity and hand strength, eye-hand coordination, tactile tolerance, and sensory awareness through proprioceptive input.

Suggested Dialogue: If the child is talking, have him say words or sentences about what he is making. Tell him to name the color, shape, object, letter, and number he is making, and to identify the tools he is using.

Additional Activities:

- Use alphabet cookie cutters and cut out the letters of his name.

- Use play dough mats to create different pictures. Have the child roll, cut, and mold to make his own creations.

- Play hide and seek using small toy animals, colored beads, or pennies hidden in the play dough.

- Use **Crayola Model Magic**, a soft, squishy modeling material, in place of play dough. This model material may be more sensory tolerated if play dough is offensive for the child to touch and handle.

- **Shape, Model, and Mold Play Set** by Melissa and Doug: Have the child identify the colors and textures of the dough. Use rolling pins and cutting tools to flatten and shape the dough. Use the wooden stamp cubes to stamp the dough.

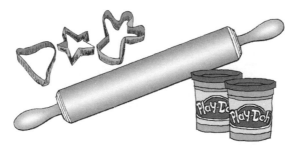

25. Arts and Crafts

Use foamies kit of shapes, letters, flowers, fish, animals, dinosaurs, and sports balls to stick or glue onto paper to make collages. Use stickers, pom-poms, feathers, glitter, and paint to make collages. Pour a small amount of glue on a plate to be used for gluing feathers and colored pom-poms onto paper to make collages and decorations. You can draw big circles, squares, other shapes, or animal shapes and have him glue various materials inside the shaped areas. Buy holiday-related crafts so he can decorate collages for all the different holidays.

Develops/Improves: Visual perception, eye-hand coordination, tactile tolerance to different textures.

Suggested Dialogue: Encourage the use of language while the child is doing an activity. Ask him how each item feels and to name each object he uses.

Additional Activities:

- Write his name and have him decorate it with glitter glue.

- Use foamies or stickers to make a collage of an ocean with sea animals, a meadow filled with flowers, or a zoo filled with animals. Have the child tell about his picture.

- Make birthday cards using foam shapes and numbers.

26. Brush and Finger Painting

Place a little finger paint on paper. Have the child choose a couple of colors he likes and have him play with the paint to get used to the feel of the paint on his fingers. Have him scribble with the finger paints. Draw a road path, simple lines and curves, shapes, letters, and numbers and have him follow with his finger. Teach him how to hold a paintbrush and paint his own masterpiece.

Develops/Improves: Fine motor skills, eye-hand coordination, grasping, tactile tolerance, and sensory awareness.

Suggested Dialogue: Engage the child in conversation about what he is doing and how it feels. Ask the child, "Do you like to paint with your fingers?" and "Tell me about your picture." While painting, you can model language by explaining in single words the motions that you are performing "up and over, down and around."

Additional Activities:

- Play "Copy Me." Paint something easy for the child to copy, i.e., a circle, happy face, sun, square, triangle, a line, or dots. If he is not able to copy your drawing, try using a hand over hand approach with the child to copy the object.

- Finger paint on different surfaces. Try finger painting with paper on an easel or a paper taped to a wall with a washable surface, such as tile in the kitchen or bathroom.

- Use **Crazy Foam** to finger paint on the bathtub wall while taking a bath.

27. Sponge Painting

Using animal, shape, and alphabet sponges have the child dip them into paint and sponge them onto paper to make a collage. When finished, let him clean the sponges with water. Have him squeeze them and get used to the paint and water on his hands.

Develops/Improves: Sensory awareness, tactile tolerance, eye-hand coordination, and hand strength and manipulation skills.

Suggested Dialogue: Ask the child to identify objects in his picture by pointing to or naming each object. Encourage him to talk about his picture. Have him express how the sponges feel and look, for example, wet and squishy or yellow and full of holes.

Additional Activities:

- Play "Match a Shape." Draw a shape and have the child sponge paint the correct shape next to it.

- Have the child sponge paint a picture of animals in a zoo. Encourage him to say a sentence about his picture.

- Sponge paint the letters in the child's name and have him copy and identify each letter.

47

28. Textured Play

Gently rub feathers, pom-poms, cotton balls, sand paper, and different textured sponges on his legs, arms, hands, belly, and back. Allow the child to get used to the different textures. This will help alleviate tactile defensiveness. Choose only one or two textures at a time so you do not over stimulate. If he finds this difficult, have him do it to himself first.

Develops/Improves: Body awareness, discrimination of touch, and desensitizing to tactile sensations.

Suggested Dialogue: Name the different parts of the child's body as you rub them. Then ask the child to name the body part you rubbed.

Additional Activities:

- Ask the child to close his eyes while you rub a feather on his arm for a few seconds. Ask the child to open his eyes and name or point to the body part you touched.

- Place several objects, i.e., a feather, pom-pom, cotton ball, sand paper, and sponge, in a bag or box with a hole cut out so the child cannot see the object. Ask him to find one of the objects by feeling around in the bag or the box and then name the object.

29. Odorless Shaving Cream/ Odorless Hand Lotion

Spray shaving cream or hand lotion onto a cookie sheet or table placemat. Have the child press his fingers and palms into the shaving cream and play with it. Have him rub his hands in it. You can draw or write letters, numbers, or make shapes in it. Drive a small toy car through it. Put shaving cream on the side of the tub for him to play with while taking a bath. Also, use soap with different textures, such as gels, foams, liquids, and hand sanitizers.

Develops/Improves: Awareness and discrimination of touch sensation, tactile tolerance, and eye-hand coordination skills.

Suggested Dialogue: Describe the feel of the textures as the child plays.

Additional Activities:

- Use whipped cream on a cookie sheet instead of shaving cream and allow the child to rub his hands in it and put his fingers in his mouth to taste the whipped cream.

- Have the child rub hand lotion into your hands. Tell the child, "This feels nice. My hands feel soft."

30. Face Painting

Using your finger, soft sponge, cotton ball, or thin paintbrush, gently paint a picture on his hand. Once he feels comfortable with this sensation, let him look into a mirror while you paint a picture on his face. This encourages the child to tolerate more sensations on his face. Begin on his cheek, and then try the chin and forehead. Increase the area on his face slowly and only do as much as he can tolerate. Once he gets used to the sensation you may eventually be able to paint his whole face.

Develops/Improves: Sensory awareness and tolerance of touch sensation.

Suggested Dialogue: Have the child look into the mirror and ask him, "What do you see on your face?"

Additional Activities:

- Place removable or washable tattoos on the child's arm, leg, or hand. Stickers may also be used.

- Have the child use a soft face brush or soft newborn hairbrush to wash off face painting from his own face.

31. Deep Body Pressure Massage/Joint Compression

Perform deep pressure and joint compression massages on arms, hands, fingers, legs, feet, toes, and back.

Develops/Improves: Provides input to tactile and proprioceptive system; calms and organizes the sensory motor systems; desensitizes and regulates the senses.

Suggested Dialogue: Name the different body parts you are massaging: "Now I am going to rub your legs. Now I am going to rub your arms. Now I am going to brush your back. Now I am going to brush your arms."

Additional Activities:

- Have an occupational therapist show you how to perform the three-step massage therapy: 1) Body Massage; 2) Brushing Technique; 3) Joint Compression. (For brushing you can use Walbarger Pressure Brush: www.pfot.com.)

- Provide a beanbag chair for the child to sit in while looking at books or watching a video.

- Ball bath: Encourage your child to move around in a tunnel filled with plastic colored balls or in a small pool filled with plastic balls.

- Sign the child up for swimming lessons or tumbling class.

- Play classical music or nursery rhymes, or sing songs during the massages.

32. Bubbles

Blow lots of bubbles all around the child and then towards him. Let him try to step on and pop the bubbles. If he is afraid, just blow a few away from him and let him observe that they will not hurt him. Have him touch, clap, chase, and stomp the bubbles. Have him try to blow the bubbles.

Develops/Improves: Awareness and tolerance of sensory sensations, oral motor skills, and body awareness.

Suggested Dialogue: Make up fun rhymes: "Bubbles, bubbles, run, run, run; lots of bubbles make lots of fun," and "Chase the bubbles and pop, pop, pop; lots of bubbles make lots of pops," as the child plays.

Additional Suggestions:

- Once the child can tolerate lots of bubbles, you can use a bubble machine or a bubble gun to shoot out bubbles. He can use the bubble gun to spray bubbles. Run, chase, and pop lots of bubbles.

- Have the child blow bubbles for you to pop.

33. Echo Mike

Let the child hold an echo mike up to his mouth. Make sure he places it so it surrounds his whole mouth. Let him blow into it. Have him make sounds, say words, sing, and hum into the mike. Use other instruments like the flute and harmonica.

Develops/Improves: Oral motor skills; alleviates oral defensiveness.

Suggested Dialogue: Say a word or short sentence to the child and have him repeat it into the echo mike. Provide the child with praise by saying, "Nice job speaking into the mike," and "This game is lots of fun."

Additional Activities:

- Have the child talk into the mike and sing a song or say a nursery rhyme.

- Have him say the alphabet or count numbers from one to ten.

- Remember to clap your hands in applause after the child's performance.

34. Party Blowers, Pinwheels, and Whistles

Have the child blow on a party blower, pinwheel, and whistle.

Develops/Improves: Oral motor skills; alleviates oral defensiveness.

Suggested Dialogue: Say to the child, "Let's pretend it's a birthday party and celebrate!"

Additional Activities:

- Play marching band with musical instruments that the child can blow into, such as a toy harmonica, flute, or saxophone.

- Purchase party blowers for all the guests at his birthday party. Have fun!

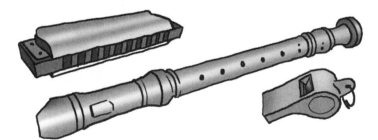

35. Feathers and Cotton Balls

Have the child blow feathers and cotton balls from the palm of your hand. Then place one in his hand and have him blow it.

Develops/Improves: Oral motor skills; alleviates oral defensiveness.

Suggested Dialogue: Tell the child if he is blowing hard or soft. Demonstrate how you can blow hard or softly and encourage him to look at your face.

Additional Activities:

- Counting game: Line up between two to ten feathers or cotton balls and have him count and blow each one.

- Play cotton ball races to see who wins by blowing their cotton ball across the finish line on a table.

36. Stamps

Use a stamp pad and a variety of stamps to stamp pictures on paper. Use stamps of animals, shapes, flowers, dinosaurs, letters, cars, and trucks. Have him sort, pattern, and count the stamps. Place his finger on the stamp pad and have him stamp his fingerprint onto the paper. Put stamps on his arms and hands.

Develops/Improves: Visual-motor discrimination, eye-hand coordination, counting, and awareness of and tolerance to tactile sensation.

Suggested Dialogue: "Tell me about your picture," and "Which stamp is your favorite?"

Additional Activities:

- Use stamps to create birthday and holiday cards.

- Have the child stamp his name on paper or a greeting card.

- Use stamps to created gift-wrapping paper. Use large easel-size paper to stamp designs onto.

37. Sticker Fun

Place a variety of stickers on paper. Use stickers of hearts, sports, shapes, balloons, animals, planets, cars, holiday themes, instruments, nature, and super heroes. Put a sticker on his hand or arm.

Develops/Improves: Eye-hand coordination, counting, and awareness of and tolerance to sensory stimuli.

Suggested Dialogue: "Tell me about your picture." Ask the child, "Do you want me to put the sticker on your hand or arm?"

Additional Suggestions:

- Make collages of different stickers.

- Make a birthday card using cake, presents, and balloons stickers.

- Sort stickers by animals, sports, and instruments and have the child place stamps in correct column.

- Pattern stickers by colors, animals, or shapes. i.e., cat, dog, horse, cat, dog, horse.

38. Holiday Foamies

Use foamies decorations during the different holidays. Use glue-on foamies to make Christmas trees, Christmas stockings, gingerbread houses, flags, hearts, Easter bunnies and eggs, Halloween masks and costumes, haunted houses, and Thanksgiving turkeys. Make holiday cards.

Develops/Improves: Fine motor, eye-hand coordination, manual dexterity, and language.

Suggested Dialogue: Encourage use of dialogue while working. Ask the child to talk about each holiday and what he does on that day.

Additional Suggestions:

- Display the child's holiday decorations in his home.

- Personalize a small picture frame with the child's favorite foamie, insert a picture of him, and give it to him as a gift.

39. View Finder

Use a viewfinder with pictures of things he likes in it. Hold it up to his eyes and let it touch his face. While he looks through it, press down on the handle so the pictures change and he can view different pictures. Once he feels comfortable, let him press down and change the pictures himself.

Develops/Improves: Sensory awareness, visual discrimination, and fine motor skills.

Suggested Dialogue: Engage the child in conversation by asking, "What are you looking at?" and "Tell me about what you see."

Additional Activities:

- Have the child look through a toy kaleidoscope, binoculars, or a telescope.

- Use an empty paper towel roll as a play telescope.

40. Candid Camera

Use a play camera with a flash to take the child's picture. If he hides his face, reassure him that the camera is fun. Let him hold the camera up to his eye and press down on the button to take your picture. Let him see how easy and fun it is. Smile for the camera.

Develops/Improves: Awareness and discrimination of visual and touch sensations, fine motor skills, and socialization.

Suggested Dialogue: Say to the child, "Smile for the picture," or "Show me a silly face."

Additional Suggestions:

- Have the child take your picture.

- Take pictures of his favorite toys and items around the house and create a book. Use one item per page and write the name of each pictured object below it.

41. Play Food

Play with pretend food. There are great visual representations of real food. Tell your child what each food item is. Have him try and say the name of the food. Have him hold a spoon and fork. Put food in pretend pots and put lids on pots. Hold the spoon and fork and place the food on plates and pretend to eat it. Store the food in containers.

Develops/Improves: Socialization, language, creativity, and fine motor skills.

Suggested Dialogue: Encourage the child to name each food item as he is playing. Ask lots of questions such as, "What fruit is this?" and the child can respond, "This is an apple."

Additional Suggestions:

- Play "Mix and Pick." Mix up the foods and tell him to pick the food you name.

- Classify the foods into food groups – fruits and vegetables.

- Color find: Ask him to pick a food item that is yellow, green, or orange. Ask him to name the color of different fruits and vegetables.

- Play pretend restaurant and ask the child to prepare an order for you, i.e., "I would like to order a banana and an apple for dessert."

- Bring the child grocery shopping. Name the items as you put them into your cart. Have him help push the cart around the store.

42. Play Picnic

Using play food and utensils, tell him that you are going on a pretend picnic. Put a towel or blanket down on the floor and have him sit and play with the food. He can put the play food in his mouth and pretend to eat. This way you can teach him the names of different foods. Have stuffed animals and/or dolls eat with him.

Develops/Improves: Language, vocabulary, eye-hand coordination, and socialization.

Suggested Dialogue: Name each food item; then have him try to name the food. Say things like, "Yummy apple!" or "Do you like the cookies?" Have him nod his head or say, "Yes." Do this with all the foods.

Additional Activities:

- Have the child pretend to cook and make lunch for you and his stuffed animals. He can tell them what he is making and have him feed his animals.

- Have a real picnic lunch with the child at the park or the beach.

43. Sand Play

Use a sand box or sand and water table. Use a bucket to construct sand castles and towers. Play with shells, cars, trucks, shovels, plastic animals, measuring cups and spoons, and other fun toys in the sand area. Have the child pour, sift, measure sand into different containers. He can smooth, pat, and rub sand. Great for sensory play – he can see how sand feels and how it can flow through his fingers.

Develops/Improves: Sensory awareness and discrimination of touch sensation touch tolerance to decrease tactile defensiveness, and eye-hand coordination skills.

Suggested Dialogue: Encourage conversation about what you are doing and ask the child questions such as, "How does the sand feel?" and "What are you making?"

Additional Suggestions:

- Use an assortment of sand molding containers to make various objects, such as animals, castles, and shapes.

- Pour sand or water into different size buckets and compare big and little.

- Use measuring cups and spoons to compare big and little.

- Go to the beach and bury the child's body in the sand. If the child is not able to tolerate his whole body, trying burying only his feet and hands.

- Use colorful **Moon Sand** mold kits to make different shapes of objects.

It is a happy talent to know how to play.

~ Ralph Waldo Emerson

Play is our brain's favorite way of learning.

~ Diane Ackerman

---

*Play gives children a chance to
practice what they are learning.*

~ Fred Rogers
American television personality (Mr. Rogers Neighborhood)

PART THREE

Fine Motor Skills

Fine motor control is the specific use of small muscles in the fingers, hands, toes, mouth, tongue, and lips. Fine motor skills include hand use, grasping, eye-hand coordination, and manual dexterity. Development of fine motor skills is necessary for activities like writing, drawing, cutting, eating, and talking.

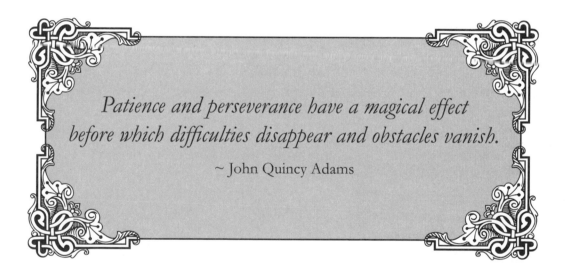

Patience and perseverance have a magical effect before which difficulties disappear and obstacles vanish.

~ John Quincy Adams

44. Tongs and Pom Poms

Use kitchen tongs to have the child pick up cotton balls and place them onto a plate. Teach him how to open and close the tongs with his thumb and pointer finger. After he can pick up cotton balls, have him pick up pom-poms. This helps prepare him for using scissors. You can teach sorting here. Sort the cotton balls from the pom-poms.

Develops/Improves: Color discrimination, eye-hand coordination, manual dexterity, and strengthens small muscles of the hand.

Suggested Dialogue: Ask the child to pick up all the blue pom-poms using the tongs and place them onto a plate. Encourage him to count the pom-poms as he places them onto a plate or into a small bowl.

Additional Activities:

- Play "Mix and Pick." Name different colored pom-pom balls for him to pick up.

- Use tongs to pattern pom-pom balls by color: yellow, green, blue, yellow, green, blue.

- Use tongs to sort pom-pom balls by color.

- Count cotton balls from one to ten.

- Use a kitchen timer and race to pick up pom-pom balls using tongs and place in a bucket. Whoever has the most wins!

- Play **Bed Bugs** (Bed Bugs is an old game and is no longer sold in stores but can be purchased on e-bay for under $10.00. It is worth it for tong practice, and it is a great game!)

- Play the **Operation** game.

- Play **Ants in the Pants** (by Hasbro).

45. Stacking Blocks and Cups

Have the child stack large blocks on top of each other. Then have him stack small blocks. Stack cups from largest to smallest and vice versa.

Develops/Improves: Eye-hand coordination, and size discrimination and sequencing skills.

Suggested Dialogue: Ask the child to point to the smallest cup or say, "Show me the big block."

Additional Activities:

- Count the cups.

- Name the colors of the cups.

- Place colored teddy bear counters into the matching colored stacking cup.

- Color matching: Build a tower of red blocks and a tower of yellow blocks.

46. Instruments

You will need a set of toy instruments: guitar, keyboard, drum, cymbals, xylophone, shakers, harmonica, tambourine, and flute. Tell him the names of all the instruments and demonstrate how to use them. Have him play them for fun. Instruments like the guitar and keyboard have colorful, easy-to-press buttons with lights, sounds, and pre-recorded songs. Have him play and sing. Play classical or children's songs on a CD and have him play instruments to the music. March, stomp around, and dance to the music.

Develops/Improves: Oral motor, gross motor and fine motor skills, auditory discrimination, language, and memory.

Suggested Dialogue: Point to different instruments and ask, "What instrument is this?" "What is your favorite?" Reply by modeling the correct responses and encourage him to repeat it.

Additional Activities:

- Tell him to close his eyes and guess which instrument you are playing. Then you close your eyes and guess which instrument he is playing.

- **Band in a Box** (Ten-piece instrument set): Includes tambourine, shakers, triangle, cymbals, etc.

47. Building Blocks

Use a variety of blocks, such as wooden, cardboard, jumbo, and pop-up blocks. Pop-up blocks fit together firmly and are great for pushing together and pulling apart. Use jumbo cardboard boxes for stacking and crashing down. They are great for construction, imaginative play, and creative thinking skills. Build houses, castles, towers, stores, and schools. Construction is another aspect of developmental praxis and allows us to put objects together in new and different ways.

Develops/Improves: Fine motor skills, eye-hand coordination, imagination, and creativity.

Suggested Dialogue: Encourage lots of conversation while the child is playing. Provide praise by saying, "Nice job building with the blocks." Encourage him to talk about what he is building.

Additional Activities:

- Have the child build his own city and neighborhood. Use a variety of types of blocks together to play and build, i.e., cardboard blocks and wooden blocks.

- Sort blocks by color and size.

- Sort blocks by size, big blocks in one pile and small blocks in another.

- Use blocks with pictures, letters, and numbers for recognition, matching, stacking, and sorting.

- Use **Beginner Pattern Blocks** (by Melissa and Doug) to teach matching, sorting, and color recognition.

- Use **Bristle Blocks** to construct buildings.

48. Puzzles

Use a variety of floor and table puzzles to teach the child about different places, objects, and things he needs to know about in his world.

Include puzzles of types of animals (pets, farm, zoo, and ocean animals), shapes, letters, numbers, parks, transportation, instruments, food, and sports. Encourage him to say and point to different puzzle pieces; then have him place them in the correct spot. Begin with single insert object puzzles.

Develops/Improves: Language, vocabulary, fine motor skills, eye-hand coordination, and spatial relations skills

Suggested Dialogue: If the child is speaking, encourage him to say a short sentence about each puzzle-piece object. If the child is not talking yet, name the object and have him point to it.

Additional Activities:

- Use peg puzzles for the child to pick up the pieces with a pincer grip and place in the correct place. (**Fish Colors Peg Puzzle** by Melissa and Doug)

- Play "Mix and Pick." Say the name of different puzzle pieces for him to find.

- Play a "Guess Who" game: "Find the animal that says 'Meow,'" or "Find a red fruit."

49. Stack and Sort Board

Sort and stack by colors, numbers, and shapes.

Develops/Improves: Eye-hand coordination, visual perception and color, number and shape discrimination, and recognition skills.

Suggested Dialogue: Ask the child how many squares there are and what color are the circles. Reply by modeling a correct response for him to repeat.

Additional Activities:

- Use **Woodshop Toys Rainbow Numbers** by Learning Resources. This 15-piece matching and stacking board teaches number, color, and shape recognition.

- Pattern blocks by colors (red, blue, red, blue) or shapes (circle, square, triangle, circle, square, triangle).

- Identify and count the different shapes.

50. Wooden Beads

Have the child string large, different-shaped wooden beads on a thick string. Have him pattern the beads by color and shapes.

Develops/Improves: Fine motor skills, eye-hand coordination, grasping, color and shape discrimination, and pattern sequencing skills.

Suggested Dialogue: Ask the child, "How many beads are on the string?" and "What color beads did you use?" If needed, model the correct response for the child to imitate.

Additional Activities:

- Pattern beads by color: yellow, green, blue, yellow, green, blue.

- Pattern beads by shapes: square, circle, square, and circle.

- Count the beads after they are strung.

- Bead It! Have the child use elastic string to string beads to make a bracelet or necklace that he can wear or give as a gift.

- **Wooden Lacing Beads** by Melissa and Doug. These particular beads have colors, shapes, and numbers. Place numbered cube beads in a row from one to ten. Ask him to string the beads in a specific order by color, shape, or number. Sequence and sort the beads.

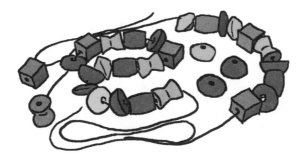

51. Snap-Beads

Push snap-beads together and pull apart. Have the child pattern snap-beads by color. Snap beads together and then connect each end to make a circle.   .

Develops/Improves: Eye-hand coordination, grasping, hand strength, sensory motor skills, color recognition, and discrimination skills.

Suggested Dialogue: Encourage lots of language by asking, "How many beads did you use?" and "What color beads did you use?"

Additional Activities:

- Tell the child the number of beads for him to count and snap together.

- Ask the child to name the different colors and design color patterns.

- Play "Beat the Clock." Set a kitchen timer and have the child snap all his beads together before the timer sounds. Start with giving him only three or four beads to snap together to "beat the clock." Increase the number of beads as his skill develops.

52. Rainbow Peg Play

Have the child stack, count, sort, and pattern pegs on the textured foam activity mat (by Learning Resources).

Develops/Improves: Fine motor skills, eye-hand coordination, visual perception, and cognitive skills.

Suggested Dialogue: Encourage the child to tell you what colors he is stacking.

Additional Activities:

- Stack pegs by color, such as all yellow in one stack.

- Stack pegs by shape, such as all squares in one stack.

- Practice counting skills using the pegs.

- Stack pegs from short to tall.

- Stacking Shapes Pegboard (by Learning Resources)

- Wooden Pound-A-Peg (by Melissa and Doug)

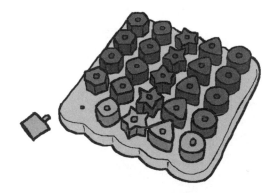

53. Coloring/ Drawing

Get simple-shape and simple-object coloring books. Have child color and scribble using various colored crayons on a blank sheet of paper. Have him color in coloring books of things he likes. Color animals, shapes, holiday pictures, flowers, and trees. From ages one to two a child holds (large) crayons with a fisted grasp. At two to three years of age, begin teaching the three-finger grasp.

Develops/Improves: Improves pre-writing skills, eye-hand coordination, grasping, and visual motor skills.

Suggested Dialogue: Tell the child the colors of the crayons and encourage him to say them. Always encourage pronunciation of the initial consonant sound, such as "b" for blue. Remind the child to color within the lines of his picture.

Additional Suggestions:

- Use large stencils to have the child practice and learn how to draw simple shapes and objects.

- Practice connecting the dots to form vertical and horizontal lines and simple shapes, such as a square, triangle, and rectangle.

- Make a simple wide, straight, or curved line maze drawn across a paper. Place a sticker at the end of the maze and encourage the child not to touch the sides of the maze as he draws his line through it.

- Practice tracing simple lines, shapes, and objects.

- Use **Magna Doodle, Doodle Pro,** or **Glow Doodle** to practice drawing and writing. These are great toys to take along on car rides.

54. Easel

Have the child color and scribble while standing at an easel. Draw a circle, square, and triangle, and vertical, horizontal, and squiggly lines, and have him copy them. Ask him to draw a specific shape. Use a hand-over-hand approach to trace a shape if the child does not attempt to copy the shape.

Develops/Improves: Strengthens postural control and visual motor skills needed for writing activities.

Suggested Dialogue: Give the child verbal cues while he is copying a line or a shape. For a vertical line say, "The line goes down," for a circle, "The circle goes around," and for a triangle, "The line goes up the hill, down the hill, and across."

Additional Activities:

- Use large stencils to draw a circle, square, triangle, and simple objects.

- Have the child connect dots to draw a vertical or horizontal line and connect the dots to draw a square or triangle.

- Show him how to draw or paint simple pictures using shapes: sun, house, animal, snowman, smiley face, flowers, trees, or ice cream cone (upside down triangle with a circle on top).

- Encourage the child to color within the lines of a picture.

- Use playground chalk to teach beginning grasping skills on a chalkboard easel.

55. Popsicle Stick Play

Make different shapes using Popsicle sticks. Have the child copy the shapes you make. Make a square, rectangle, cross, triangle, star, or house, using parallel, horizontal, and vertical lines. Ask him to name the shapes. Once he learns how to make these, have him do it on his own.

Develops/Improves: Visual motor skills, eye-hand coordination, thinking, and imitation skills

Suggested Dialogue: Encourage the child to name the shapes he is making. Provide praise by saying, "Nice job! You made a triangle."

Additional Activities:

- Pattern colored Popsicle sticks – red, blue, purple, red, blue, purple – for the child to copy.

- Count sticks from one to ten.

- Play "Simon Says" with Popsicle sticks. "Simon says to make a square."

56. Cutting Wooden Fruit Velcro Play Food (by Melissa and Doug)

Use the wooden knife to have the child cut each piece of fruit and name it. Fruits can either be cut into halves, thirds, or fourths.

Develops/Improves: Eye-hand coordination and beginning math concepts.

Suggested Dialogue: Provide praise to the child by saying, "Nice job cutting the apple." Ask him to count how many pieces he now has.

Additional Activities:

- Play with other Melissa and Doug food sets, such as **Wooden Cookie Set, Pizza Party Set, Ice Cream Parlor Set,** and **Birthday Cake Set.**

- Use the **Wooden Cookie Set** to have the child sort the cookie toppings by color. Use a wooden knife to slice the cookies and then count them. Teach him how to use a spatula to place cookies onto a cookie sheet. Have him put on an oven mitt and pretend to bake in the oven.

- Use the **Pizza Party Set** wooden knife to cut pizza slices. Count the number of slices.

- Use the **Ice Cream Parlor Set**. Have the child use the plastic scoop and stack different flavored play ice cream onto a wooden cone. Teach the names of the four flavors so the child can identify each one.

- Use the **Birthday Cake Set** to decorate the cake. Use the wooden knife to cut slices of cake and place them on a plate.

- Have the child measure, pour, and stir ingredients with adult assistance to bake cupcakes.

57. Scissor Skills

Use small plastic children's scissors (#4) to have the child cut along a straight line or simple curve. If he has trouble with scissors, continue practicing with the tongs and pom-poms.

Develops/Improves: Eye-hand coordination and strengthens hand muscles.

Suggested Dialogue: Encourage conversation about what the child is doing by saying, "Nice job cutting on the line."

Additional Activities:

- If the child cannot use scissors, practice tearing strips of paper. These pieces of confetti may be used to decorate the table for dinner.

- Try using loop scissors if the child is having difficulty controlling and cutting with scissors.

- Cut out pictures from magazines and create a collage picture.

- Cut out store coupons from the newspaper.

58. Lace Pictures

Have the child lace string around different pictures. Have him put string in the hole and pull it up the other side.

Develops/Improves: Eye-hand coordination, grasping, and visual perception.

Suggested Dialogue: Talk to the child while he is playing. Say to him, "You are lacing a truck. Nice job lacing."

Additional Activities:

- Punch holes around the edge of large foamies and lace to create holiday decorations or picture frames.

- Have the child lace a play shoe. With a marker, color one of the shoe strings red or blue so it will be easier for the child to learn to tie his shoe.

- Practice lacing with the **Learn to Lace and Tie Shoe** by Melissa and Doug.

- **One, Two, Tie My Shoe** by Alex.

- Lace puppets. (www.sensoryinterventions.com)

59. Geoboard

Designs are made on the geoboard by stretching rubber bands on a grid of pegs until the desired shape is formed. Help the child identify and make simple geometric shapes. Begin by making a straight line, then an angle. Make a triangle, square, rectangle, and diamond and have him copy you. Teach size and shape.

Develops/Improves: Visual perception, spatial relationships, eye-hand coordination, and manual dexterity skills.

Suggested Dialogue: Ask the child to copy your design. Say, "This is a triangle," or "This is a square."

Additional Activities:

- Provide help to the child as needed to manipulate the rubber bands over the pegs to form the correct shape.

- Use multicolored rubber bands and create designs.

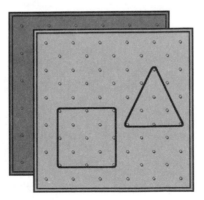

60. Snapping/Buttoning/Zipping Board Puzzle

Use a puzzle with snaps, buttons, and zippers. Teach the child how to snap, button, zip, and buckle clothing articles on a puzzle.

Develops/Improves: Fine motor skills, dexterity, and sensory motor awareness.

Suggested Dialogue: Encourage the child to tell you what fastener he is using.

Additional Activities:

- Have the child practice garment fastenings (snap, lace, buckle, zip and tie) on a **Learn to Dress Jake** doll, **Dressy Bessie** doll, or **Dapper Dan** doll. (See appendix to purchase)

- **Basic Skills Board Teddy Bear Puzzle** (by Melissa and Doug): Have the child snap, button, buckle, zip, lace, and tie pieces on a teddy bear puzzle. Have him name each skill and name the color of each puzzle piece.

- Use **Latches Board** (by Melissa and Doug): Open a variety of latches on doors and windows on a house to see colorful animals behind them. Have the child identify the colors on the doors, the animals behind the doors, and to count how many animals are behind the doors.

- Use dress-up clothing and costumes to have the child practice zipping up a jacket and buttoning a shirt.

61. Costumes/Dress-Up

Using a variety of costumes that have head and face components, have the child put different hats on his head and masks over his face. Use a baseball cap, cowboy hat, surgeon's cap, fireman's helmet, builder's hardhat and goggles, super-hero masks, and play sunglasses. If he resists, just hold it over his head and lightly touch his head. Do  this over and over until he allows you to put it on his head. Use the same technique to get him to put things on his face. First model putting on the clothes, then have him dress up in front of the mirror. Practice a variety of garment fastenings on the dress-up clothes.

Develops/Improves: Creativity, imagination, dexterity, body awareness, and motor planning skills.

Suggested Dialogue: Encourage lots of dialogue by asking the child, "What are your wearing?" and "Who do you look like?"

Additional Activities:

- Have the child dress up and act out a simple play.

- Let the child pretend he is a fireman and use the rope as a hose to put out the fire.

- Visit the fire station with the child.

62. Work Bench

Have the child build with his own toy workbench. Have him name and use a variety of tools, such as hammer, saw, power drill, screwdriver, screws, drill, nuts, bolts, and ruler. Use tools to build houses with blocks. It is great for fine motor development to drill, screw, and unscrew nuts and bolts, and it helps develop a pincer grip.

Develops/Improves: Fine motor skills, eye-hand coordination, grasping, manual dexterity, sensory motor skills, language, and imaginative play.

Suggested Dialogue: Ask the child to tell you what tool he is using and what he is building.

Additional Activities:

- Let the child pretend to saw, hammer, and nail blocks together to make stores, houses, and buildings.

- Use **Little Tikes Discover Sounds** Tools (drill, screwdriver, and hammer). Have the child pretend to repair items in the home, such as a table, cabinet, or the floor.

- Use the **Handy Mandy Talkin' Toolbox.** Watch the *Handy Manny* television program or video to encourage the child's interest in tools before using a workbench and tools.

PART FOUR

Gross motor skills involve large muscle movement in the arms, legs, and trunk for developing and enhancing the motor coordination necessary for walking, running, jumping, and climbing. Gross motor activities stimulate and encourage development of the vestibular and proprioceptive systems, motor planning skills, body awareness, visual spatial skills, and bilateral coordination.

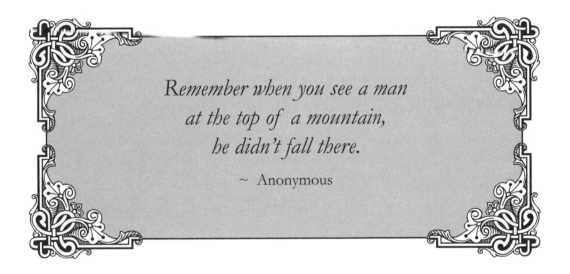

Remember when you see a man
at the top of a mountain,
he didn't fall there.

~ Anonymous

63. Obstacle Course

The obstacle course should be designed to practice many kinds of movements, such as crawling, jumping, and balancing. Pick and choose what things you want in your obstacle course. 1) Crawl under a tunnel; 2) Walk across a floor balance beam (2 x 4 or 2 x 6 board); 3) Do a forward somersault; 4) Scoot under a small table; 5) Place a hula-hoop on the floor and jump in and out of the hoop; 6) Roll across a small floor mat; 7) Climb over a stack of three couch pillows; 8) Pick up a small ball and make a basket into basketball net (2-3 feet high net); 9) Roll a ball into a set of bowling pins. Practice each of these activities in isolation before combining them into an obstacle course.

Develops/Improves: Gross motor skills, body awareness, balance, spatial relationships, and problem solving. Integrates tactile, vestibular, proprioception,[1] and visual sensations

Suggested Dialogue: Demonstrate the action requested of the child, such as crawling through the tunnel. Then say to the child, "Crawl through the tunnel." Do the same for a floor balance beam and pretend that you might fall into the water. Say, "Be careful, don't fall into the water!" as the child walks to the end of the balance beam.

Additional Activities:

- Hold the child's hand and practice walking (forward, sideways, and backwards) on a floor balance beam if he is having difficulty by himself. This applies to all of the obstacle course skills.

- Encourage riding of a tricycle or **Big Wheel** tricycle; push from behind to get the child familiar with the desired movement.

- Encourage the child to play and move around in a ball bath.

- Visit school playgrounds often to practice movement skills.

- Sign the child up for a beginner tumbling or gymnastics class or swimming lessons at the local YMCA or YWCA.

---

1 Proprioception is the ability to sense the position and location and orientation and movement of the body and its parts.

64. Park Therapy and Playground Play

Have the child swing, slide, go under a tunnel, climb up a fake rock-climb, hang from a monkey bar, and use the jump-off apparatus. Model all the activities first. If he sees that you have fun doing them and that there is nothing to be afraid of, then he will follow. Hold his hand during all activities until he feels safe. Once he feels safe, then he will be able to do it.

Develops/Improves: Sensory motor skills, vestibular and proprioception systems, gross motor skills, endurance, and strengthening of large muscle groups.

Suggested Dialogue: Encourage conversation about what you are doing and ask the child questions, such as, "Do you want me to push you more on the swing?" or "Do you want to go down the slide?" Always praise the child for his efforts saying, "Nice job swinging (or sliding, or jumping)."

Additional Activities:

- Teach the child how to jog slowly around the park.

- Ask the child to run 20-yard sprints from one marked area to another, i.e., run from the swing to the fence. Running is great exercise for all children and this will help tire him out and sleep better at night. Try to jog several days a week for about five to ten minutes.

- Take afternoon walks around the neighborhood and engage in lots of conversation.

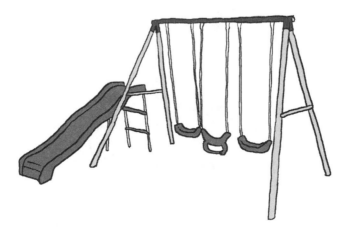

65. Mini-Trampoline

Have the child jump on the trampoline. Bounce around and sing different songs or listen to music.

Develops/Improves: Gross motor skills, balance, coordination, vestibular and proprioception systems, gravitational security, and language.

Suggested Dialogue: Encourage conversation while the child is jumping. Ask him if he is having fun or if he wants to jump higher.

Additional Activities:

- Hold on to the child's two hands if he is afraid or having difficulty jumping on the trampoline.

- Count from one to ten as you jump, then take a break and jump again.

- Say the alphabet while jumping.

66. Ball Play

Sit on the floor with the child in front of you. Roll the ball to him and have him roll the ball back to you. Both of you stand up, then gently toss a ball and try to have him catch it. Show him how to toss it back to you. Begin with the underhand throw; later try the overhand throw.

Develops/Improves: Eye-hand coordination, bilateral coordination, visual tracking, following directions, and attention to task.

Suggested Dialogue: Tell him to say, "Roll ball," "Throw ball," and "Catch ball." Ask the child to put out his hands so he can catch the ball. Say, "Ready, catch," to help the child prepare for what he is to do.

Additional Activities:

- Teach the child how to bounce a ball. Start with a large size ball that is lightweight.

- Teach the child how to throw the ball up above his head and catch it.

- Counting: Bounce the ball five to ten times and count together.

- Throw beanbags into a bucket or through a target.

67. Tunnel Fun

Have the child crawl through a play tunnel or tunnel tent. He can bring his favorite animals or toy to play with inside. You can crawl in with him and sing songs or play. Have a pretend picnic in the tent area. Tunnel play can be done at home or at the park.

Develops/Improves: Gross motor skills, coordination, body awareness, and spatial relations. Also provides joint compression and weight bearing on shoulder girdle.

Suggested Dialogue: Teach the child positional words (over, under, through, behind) by saying to him, "You are crawling *through* the tunnel," and "You can bring your animals *into* the tunnel. That will be fun."

Additional Activities:

- Roll a ball into the tunnel and have the child chase it.

- If the child is not afraid to be in the tunnel, you can roll the tunnel from side to side for the child to experience additional movement.

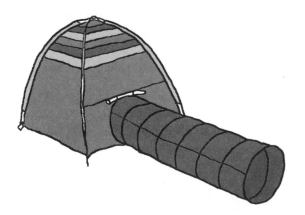

68. Tummy Time

Place a pillow under your child's belly so he is lying up on an incline.

Have him do a variety of skills from this position. Place toys in front of him and let him play with them while he is lying on an incline. This position makes him use his arms more and increases weight bearing on the shoulder girdle (chest area). Stack up two or three couch pillows and have him crawl over them.

Develops/Improves: Body awareness, strengthening of shoulder girdle, gravitational security, and self-calming.

Suggested Dialogue: Tell the child he is making his muscles strong while being on his tummy. Encourage him to do this for five- to ten-minute periods throughout the day.

Additional Activities:

- Encourage the child to remain on his tummy with the incline pillow or support himself on four arms in the tummy position while watching his favorite television show or video.

- Play on a scooter board using his hands to push and move around while on his tummy.

69. Copy Me

Teach all the different body parts. While standing in front of the child, touch a part of your body and tell him to copy you. Point to different parts of your body and rhythmically say, "Touch your head, nose, mouth, toes, cheeks, belly, leg, roll your hands, raise your arms, turn around, clap your hands, jump up and down, march in place, wave your hands, touch your cheeks, stick out your tongue, wriggle fingers, shake head back and forth and up and down, and make silly sounds." Then tell him to say and point to the body parts and you copy him.

Develops/Improves: Body awareness, motor planning, auditory discrimination, language skills, and eye-hand coordination.

Suggested Dialogue: Praise the child for touching correct body parts saying, "Nice job touching your head, nose, mouth, or toes."

Additional Activities:

- Sing "Head, Shoulders, Knees, and Toes."

- Play "Simon Says." Use the child's name, i.e., "Johnny says...."

70. Kickball

Roll the ball and have the child kick it to you. Have him run and kick a ball.

Develops/Improves: Gross motor skills, balance and bilateral coordination skills. Strengthens large muscles.

Suggested Dialogue: Remind the child to look at the ball with his eyes. Provide praise by saying, "Nice job looking at/kicking the ball." Use this opportunity to teach the child to take turns with you to kick the ball.

Additional Activities:

- Set up two cones and have the child kick a ball between the cones.

- Play soccer using a goal net to score. Count the number of times the child makes a goal.

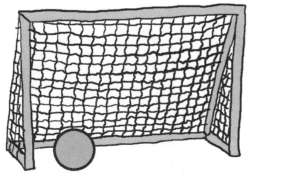

71. Hoop It Up

Use a small youth basketball and basketball hoop and have the child place the ball into the hoop to make a basket. Model and teach him how to toss a basketball into the hoop. Begin by shooting it underhand. Once he is able to place it in, step back away from the hoop and try to have him shoot it in. He can toss it in underhand or overhand.

Develops/Improves: Strengthening of shoulder girdle, eye-hand coordination, visual-spatial skills, gross motor coordination, and motor planning skills.

Suggested Dialogue: Encourage conversation while playing, such as "Try and make a basket," or "You made a basket! Great job!"

Additional Activities:

- Counting: Shoot between one and five baskets. Count aloud how many baskets he makes.

- Bouncing: Teach the child how to bounce (drop and catch the ball) and dribble a basketball. Have him bounce three times and then toss it into the basket.

- If this is too difficult, encourage the child to toss a large foam ball into a laundry basket.

72. Bowling

Roll a ball into pins to knock them over. You and the child set them back up again. Take turns bowling. This activity is great for learning how to take turns and compete.

Develops/Improves: Gross motor coordination, visual-spatial awareness, eye-hand coordination, motor planning, and socialization.

Suggested Dialogue: Encourage conversation while bowling, such as "Roll the ball and try to knock down the pins." Count how many pins the child knocks down each time. "You knocked down four pins. Good job. Try it again."

Additional Activities:

- Use a beach ball to knock over the pins. This time all the pins should fall down. This should be fun for him.

- If ten pins are too many, try using three or six pins.

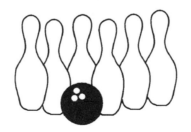

73. Hula-Hoops

Place three or four hula-hoops on the floor and have the child jump in and out of a hoop. Then have him hop from hoop to hoop. Go in one direction, then the other.

Develops/Improves: Gross motor skills, jumping, body awareness, coordination, and balance.

Suggested Dialogue: Say to the child, "Jump, use your two feet, jump in or jump out, or jump forward."

Additional Activities:

- Count the number of hoops the child jumps into.

- Play a simple hopscotch game; use one foot to hop into a hoop and then bend over to pick up an object or toy.

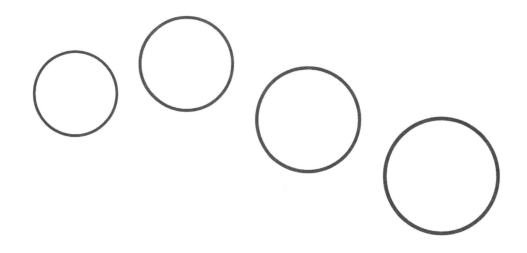

74. Therapy Ball

Using a large therapy ball, hold him and bounce him up and down on the ball. Lay him on the floor and, with consistent firm pressure, roll and press the ball up and down all over his body; this helps calm the over-stimulated child.

Develops/Improves: Body awareness, trunk control and strength, and sensory regulation.

Suggested Dialogue: Tell the child what you are doing while you are doing it. "I am bouncing the ball up and down," or "I am rolling the ball over your legs, tummy, and arms."

Additional Activity:

- Use a small size therapy ball and encourage the child to balance and sit on the ball like he would on a chair.

75. Beanbag Toss

Throw beanbags into a laundry basket. As the child's aim gets better, move farther back and throw them again. Teach him how to throw underhand and then throw overhand.

Develops/Improves: Eye-hand coordination and body awareness. Strengthens trunk and shoulder girdle.

Suggested Dialogue: Provide praise to the child by saying, "Nice job throwing the bean bags."

Additional Activities:

- Play "Catch the Beanbags." Stand close together and toss the beanbag to him so he can try and catch it. Have him toss it back to you.

- Use colored beanbags and have the child name the colors.

- Counting: Throw the beanbags into the basket five to ten times. Count aloud as the child throws the beanbags.

76. Ring Toss

Teach your child how to toss the rings onto the sticks. Begin by placing the rings onto the sticks. As his aim gets better, move farther back and throw them again.

Develops/Improves: Eye-hand coordination and body awareness. Strengthens trunk and shoulder girdle

Suggested Dialogue: Encourage the child's accuracy by saying, "Throw the ring a little harder," or "Throw the ring a little softer."

Additional Activities:

- Stand very close to the rings so some of them will go on. He can place them on if he continues to miss.

- Give the child a different amount of rings to throw each time. Have him count each ring as it is thrown. Have him say how many rings he throws each time.

- Play a horseshoe game outside on the lawn or at the beach.

77. Flashlight Fun

Shine a flashlight on different objects and toys. Hide the light and show it again. Shine the flashlight on different parts of his body and have him say what body part it is. Let your child hold his own flashlight with both hands and shine it on the wall, ceiling, and floor. Quickly move the light from spot to spot to see if he can follow. Then slowly move the light across a wall, keeping his head still and encouraging him to follow it with his eyes.

Develops/Improves: Tracking and visual motor skills.

Suggested Dialogue: Encourage the child to keep his head still by saying, "Look with your eyes." "Tell me, where is the light?" and "Is it on your hand or your foot?"

Additional Activities:

- Play "Flashlight Tag" on the wall. Have the child follow your flashlight on the wall to tag you. Praise the child by saying, "You got me!" Go as fast or as slow as the child is able to do successfully.

- Take a short walk together at night and use your flashlight to light your path.

78. The Little Gym

Enroll in your community's toddler, preschool, or kindergarten athletic programs to help develop strength, balance, flexibility, and gross motor coordination. Learn basic gymnastic, tumbling, and sports skills.

Develops/Improves: Gross motor skills, coordination, motor planning, balance, body awareness, and socialization.

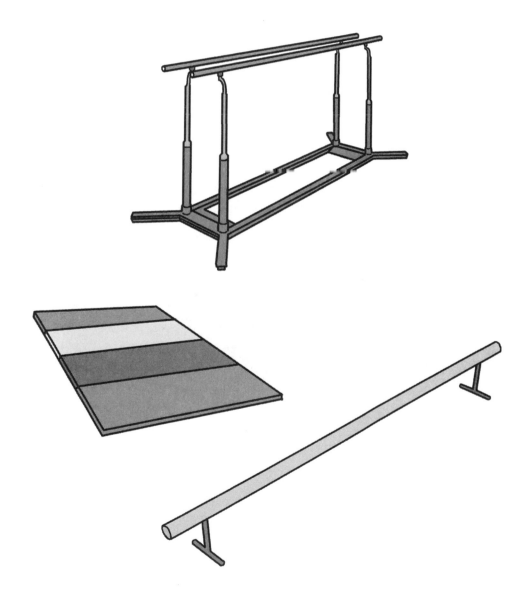

79. Swim Lessons

Enroll in swim lessons in your community so the child can learn how to swim. If your child is afraid of putting his head under water, be sure to have pre-swimming prep time. One month prior to swim lessons take handfuls of water and drip it on his head while he is taking a bath. This will allow him to get used to water coming down on his face. Once he is comfortable with that, pour a cupful of water on his head. This will help desensitize any fears that he has of water on his face. Have your child blow bubbles in the bathtub to get him used to partially putting his face in the water.

Develop/Improves: Gross motor skills, bilateral motor coordination, muscle strength, organization of sensory motor systems, and socialization.

PART FIVE

Concept Skills

At three years of age you can begin introducing your child to different concept skills for pre-k and kindergarten. Purchase preschool workbooks. Use flashcards and game cards to introduce concepts such as same and different, sequencing, opposites, big and small, rhyming, and matching. For math, teach counting, sorting, patterning, and numbers. Pre-reading skills include identifying letters and letter sounds. Also teach the seasons, days of the week, and months of the year. Writing skills include copying shapes, (circle, square, triangle), tracing, coloring, and learning to print their name.

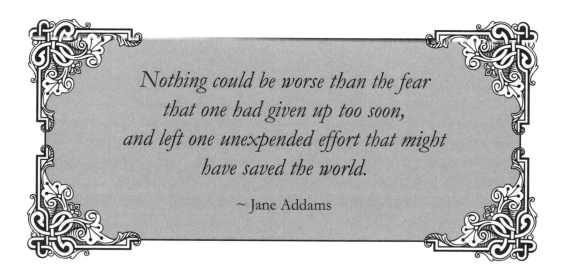

Nothing could be worse than the fear that one had given up too soon, and left one unexpended effort that might have saved the world.

~ Jane Addams

80. Same and Different

Use objects to teach the concept of "same and different." Put three to four items of the same object in a row and make one object different. For example, put three blocks and one car in a row. Say, "These three blocks are the same. The car is different." Put four balls and one stuffed animal in a row. Say, "These four balls are the same. The stuffed animal is different." Teach him to classify the objects by explaining why some of the items are the same and one is different.

Develops/Improves: Preschool and kindergarten concepts same and different.

Suggested Dialogue: Show the child three red blocks and ask him if they are the same or different. Reply, "They are the same because they are all red blocks."

Additional Activities:

- Classify objects by size, shape, or color.

- Have the child explain why three are the same and the other one is different. Use objects like marbles, pom-poms, balls, crayons, fruit, blocks, or teddy bears

81. Sequence Cards

Place three-piece pictures of everyday activities and routines in sequence. Instruct the child to describe which goes first, next, and last in order. Encourage him to use complete sentences. Remember, to elicit language, you will have to ask questions. The child may need some explanation of the pictures at first. Keep in mind that you are giving the child the tools of language while explaining the sequence cards.

Develops/Improves: Language, thinking, and visual sequencing skills, and story telling.

Suggested Dialogue: If needed, assist the child by explaining to him what is happening in the first picture, and give him additional cues as needed for the second and third cards. Ask the child questions about each sequence card.

Additional Activities:

- Place the first card of the sequence down and encourage the child to tell you what comes next. Have him tell you what activity the person is doing. If he is not able to express it, tell him what the activity is and have him repeat it. If the child does not talk, have him point and then place the pictures in the correct order.

- Use four-, five- and six-piece sequence cards after they have mastered the three-piece sequencing cards.

82. Shape Sorting Clock

Teach the child the concept of telling time on a clock. Have him name some of the different shapes and place the twelve different shapes into their correct slots on the clock.

Develops/Improves: Shape and number recognition, and telling time.

Suggested Dialogue: Explain the concept of morning, afternoon, and night, and how a clock is used to tell time. Say to the child, "You eat breakfast at eight in the morning, lunch at noon, and supper at six in the evening."

Additional Activities:

- Ask the child to line up the pieces in numerical order. Begin with only a few numbers and build up to one through twelve.

83. Weather Chart

Use a weather chart to teach the child the different kinds of weather. Show pictures of weather: sunny, rainy, snowy, cloudy, hot, and cold.

Develops/Improves: Preschool and kindergarten concepts, and awareness of the child's environment.

Suggested Dialogue: Ask the child to tell you what the weather is today. Say, "Is it sunny or rainy?" Ask the child if he would need boots and an umbrella for a sunny day or a rainy day.

Additional Activities:

- Explain that in different months of the year you have different kinds of weather.

- Tell him the month and have him point to the type of weather that usually occurs in that month. "In January it is cold. Where is the picture that shows it is cold?"

- Point to pictures in a book and ask the child if it is a sunny, cloudy, or snowy day.

84. Magnetic Calendar

Use a child-themed magnetic calendar to teach days of the week and months of the year. Explain that there are seven days in a week and twelve months in a year.

Develops/Improves: Preschool and kindergarten concepts and organizational skills.

Suggested Dialogue: Tell the child, "Today is (name the day)." Encourage him to repeat, "Today is…." Do the same for each month. Say, "Your birthday is in (name the month)," or "Halloween is in October."

Additional Activities:

- Cross off each day on the calendar.

- Place holiday stickers on the child's calendar on the appropriate dates.

- Write down the days of the week and have him count them.

- Write down the months of the year and have him count them.

PART SIX

Self-Care/Activities of Daily Living

Self-care activities include feeding, dressing, bathing, toileting and personal hygiene. Independence in self-care skills encourages a child to function more independently in his home and school environment. It also includes the development of social skills to function appropriately in all activities of daily living such as attending friend and family social gatherings, shopping, and going to a restaurant.

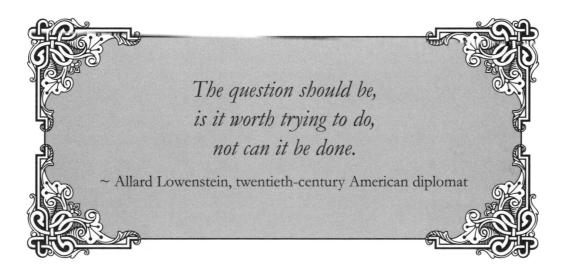

The question should be,
is it worth trying to do,
not can it be done.

~ Allard Lowenstein, twentieth-century American diplomat

85. Dressing Activities

During daily dressing activities it is a wonderful time to practice with a child naming and identifying body parts and clothing items. Practice in front of a mirror so that the child is able to see himself. It is easier for a child to learn how to take off garments such as his socks, his shirt, and his pants than it is to put on these items. Therefore, undressing is a good place to start learning these skills. Allow the child to actively assist and provide hand-over-hand assistance only as needed. Encourage the child to dress and undress himself to promote increased independence in dressing skills. If the child is tactilely defensive, clothing tags and certain textures and styles of clothing may be difficult for him to tolerate wearing. Loose-fitting clothing such as tee shirts and jogging outfits may be more comfortable. Remove tags from inside garments to allow the child to be more comfortable throughout the day.

Develops/Improves: Vocabulary, body awareness, and sensory awareness.

Suggested Dialogue: Say to the child, " Show me your feet" and then tell him that his socks and shoes go on his feet. Then ask the child, "What do you wear on your head?" If the child does not reply, model the response for him "You wear a hat on your head." Use this format for all clothing items and body parts.

Additional Activities:

- Encourage the child to wash his hands, comb his hair, and brush his teeth. Try a child-size electric toothbrush for fun!

- Play "Piggy Toes" before putting his socks on and after removing his socks.

- Practice garment fastenings on **Basic Skills Board** (by Melissa and Doug), **Dressy Bessy** or **Dapper Dan** doll. Start with learning snaps, zippers, and Velcro closures.

- Have a trunk or large box filled with dress-up clothes for fun play. Use loose-fitting clothing items such as old Halloween costumes, hats, belts, and beads.

86. Riding in a Car

There are so many learning activities that the child can engage in while riding in a car, such as language, sensory, and fine-motor skills. Be sure to have your *"goodie bag of toys for the car"* for the child to focus on and play with such as plush toys, board books, touch and feel books, toy keys, toy phone, squeezums, shakers, and hand fidgets. (See Appendix I for "goody bag of toys for the car.")

Develops/Improves: Language, attention span, and self-control.

Suggested Dialogue: Engage in conversation with your child about the things you see around you. For example, "There is the McDonald sign." At the traffic light say, "Red means stop; green means go." If he becomes distracted or bored, remind him to take out a toy from his goodie bag such as his toy phone. Say, "Talk on your toy phone." "Can you squeeze the ball?" "Look at the wonderful book." "What do you see on the viewfinder?"

Additional Activities:

- Have him draw you a picture on his magna doodle. Then praise him for his beautiful masterpiece.

- Have him try to put all the shapes in the plush shape sorter.

- Listen to books on CD's.

- Play children's song on CD's such as **Baby Beluga** (by Raffi), **Wee Sing,** and **Baby Einstein.**

87. Restaurant Activities

Practice play-eating at a restaurant, at home, or in school and reward the child by taking him to the restaurant. Initially, visit a fast food restaurant, preferably one with a child's play area to reward him after he sits and eats. Go around mid afternoon (between 2 and 3) when it is empty so you will not bother the customers. Teach the child to sit in a booth and eat properly in a restaurant without fussing, moving things around on the table, or getting up and running around. Bring your "goody bag of toys for mealtime" so he can focus and play with something while eating his food. Place a timer on the table and explain to him that he has to remain seated and eat for at least 2-3 minutes. (Increase the time sitting as you practice each week). When the timer goes off he can get up from the booth and you can take him to the play section of the restaurant.

Develops/Improves: Social skills, self-control, and mealtime etiquette.

Suggested Dialogue: Remind the child that he must stay in his seat to eat. Begin with small amounts of food that he likes, so he does not have to sit for too long. Say the child's name, "*Paul* sit down next to mommy and eat your food. You cannot get up from the table until you eat your food. When you finish eating I will take you to the play area and you can play." If he fusses, cries, or tantrums put him in a time out chair somewhere in the restaurant where there are NO customers. Redirect him back to the table to eat his food. Praise him after he has eaten and go have fun in play land.

Additional Activities:

- Have a friend or relative come over for a play date for lunch.

88. Grocery Shopping

While shopping in the food store practice naming and identifying food items such as milk, eggs, apples, bananas, and vegetables. Have the child say or point to different items that he knows when going down the aisle. Bring a snack for him to eat. Allow the child to select his favorite box of cookies to bring home. To keep your child occupied, bring a small book or hand toy.

Develops/Improves: Vocabulary and social skills.

Suggested Dialogue: Remind the child to remain seated in the cart.

Additional Activities:

- Allow the child to put away simple food items such as a box of cereal.

- Play grocery shopping at home. Identify food items from the play food.

- Divide items into food groups such as fruits, vegetables, and meats. Classify foods into groups according to shape, color, or taste.

89. Bath Time Fun

Taking a bath is a great soothing activity before bedtime. Let your child play with tub toys, splash, and enjoy the water. Let him blow bubbles in the tub or have bubble baths. He can use crazy foam, bathtub crayons, and paint to draw on the side of the tub. Use bathtub alphabet letters to reinforce alphabet learning.

Develops/Improves: Sensory motor, grasping, and eye-hand coordination.

Suggested Dialogue: Tell the child that it is bath time. Try to set up a consistent routine of giving him a bath around the same time everyday. At the end of bath time say, "All clean, all done."

Additional Activities:

- Use foam shapes and **Rub-a-Dub** stickers on the side of the bathtub to create a picture. Encourage the child to name the foam shape or object on the sticker.

- Have the child pretend to shave himself using the **Rub-a-Dub Shaving in the Tub**.

- Practice pouring skills using different size cups.

- Play with **Tub Tunes** musical instruments – piano, xylophone, drum, and flute.

- Practice counting numbers and alphabet skills in the tub. Use foam alphabet letters and numbers, or **Count Out Loud** numbers for the tub.

- Give the child the letters of his name and have him place them in correct order to spell his name on the tub wall.

- **Sesame Street Tub Pots and Pans** by Fisher Price: Kitchen supplies for the bathtub.

- Use bathtub finger-paints and crayons so he can paint and draw on the bathtub walls or on his body.

- Practice singing songs and rhyming words while he is in the tub.

- **Rub-a-Dub Dunk & Score** by Alex: A bathtub basketball game for three- and four-year-olds.

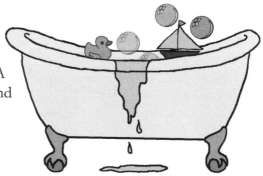

90. Bedtime Snuggles and Buggles

Tell your child it is time to "snuggle and buggle." This is my endearing term for snuggling and cuddling on the bed. Snuggle up in bed or on a couch and read a bedtime story to him. You do not need to do any skills with this; you are only reading for his listening pleasure. You can allow him to pick the book. This is a great way for both of you to wind down and become calm, quiet, and peaceful before he goes to sleep.

Develops/Improves: Language and sensory motor organization (snuggling).

Suggested Dialogue: Encourage conversation by reflecting on all the wonderful things your child did that day. Tell him to think about happy thoughts and to go right to sleep so he will have lots of energy for the next day. Remember to say, "I love you!"

Additional Activities:

- Sing a calming good night song together before he goes to sleep.

- Use a **Sound Spa** (by Homedics) for the child who has difficulty falling asleep and/or remaining asleep through the night. This helps to block out other noises so the child can have a good night sleep. Introduce the different sounds such as wind, rain, waterfall, and the ocean on the sound machine to determine which one he prefers listening to. Select a calming, peaceful, and familiar sound such as the wind. Some children may be sensitive to sounds and may not like the sound at first. Play the different sounds throughout the day to get the child familiar to the sounds. Make sure the child feels comfortable and likes a particular sound before using it at bedtime. (Available at Bed, Bath and Beyond)

Appendix I

Toys and Supplies for Skills and Drills Program

This is a list of suggested toys to be used to implement the Skills and Drills program. Not every toy needs to be purchased, pick and choose the ones that are most appropriate for your child's specific needs.

The toys used for the original 78 Skills and Drills with Roman are noted with an asterisk.

Language Skill Toys
- Alphabet letters*
- Numbers one through nine*
- Touch and Feel books*
- Flashcards (objects, matching, opposites)*
- Activity picture cards*
- Puzzles (shapes, alphabet, numbers, animals)*
- Shape sorter*
- Play food*
- Toy cell phone*
- View finder*
- Toy camera*
- Kits for imaginative play (farm, doctor, circus, nurse, builder, tea party)*
- Multi-colored balloon poster board*
- Children's/toddler's picture books*
- Coloring books*
- Puppets*
- Colored teddy bear counters
- **Touch and Feel** activity cards (DK or Hands-On-Learning by Scholastic)
- Felt Tales story boards (www.sensoryinterventions.com)
- **Touch and Feel** animal books
- Fisher Price *Story Book Rhymes*
- Shapes and color **Touch and Feel** picture cards (by DK)
- Circle, square, and triangle **Large Knob Puzzle** (by Melissa and Doug)
- **Jumbo House Knob Puzzle** (First Shapes by Melissa and Doug)
  Eight-Piece **Shapes Jumbo Puzzle** (by Melissa and Doug)
- **Candy Land Castle** game
- **Twister** game
- Toy walkie-talkies
- **My First Numbers** and **Counting Touch and Feel** picture cards (by DK)
- **Fridge Phonics**
- **Baby Einstein Alphabooks**

- Colored teddy bears counters
- Shape sorter clock
- Association cards
- Sequencing cards
- Classifying cards
- Rhyming cards
- Emotional flash cards
- Opposite cards
- Large foam floor alphabet puzzle
- ABC One Inch Blocks by Melissa and Doug
- Step Two Puppet Theater
- Medical Kit by Fisher Price

Sensory Skill Toys
- Play dough*
- Animal shapes cutters*
- Bubbles*
- Foamies kits*
- Arts and craft supplies: stickers, pom-poms, cotton balls, feathers, glitter glue*
- Construction paper*
- Washable crayons and markers*
- Washable finger paint*
- Washable sponge paint*
- Paint brushes*
- Shaving cream*
- Echo mike*
- Party blowers*
- Plastic whistles/pinwheels*
- Stamps*
- Stickers*
- View finder*
- Toy camera*
- Play food*
- Sandbox/table*
- Party blowers, whistles, flute, harmonica*
- Toy camera/binoculars*
- Plastic fruit*
- Toy musical instruments*
- **Moon Sand**/sand toys
- Kaleidoscope
- Binoculars
- Small plastic colored balls
- Beanbag chair

- Washable tattoos
- Hand lotion
- Shaving cream
- Bathtub finger paint
- Sand paper
- Classical music CD
- Picnic basket
- Face brush/newborn hair brush
- Sensory Balls by Imaginarium
- Disc Swing by Little Tykes
- Crayola Model Magic

Fine Motor Skill Toys
- Stack and sort board*
- Rainbow peg play*
- Toy instruments*
- Blocks (wood, cardboard, pop-up blocks, etc.)*
- Arts and craft supplies: finger paint, paint, paint brushes, washable markers, crayons, scissors, cotton balls, pom-poms, foamies, shaving cream, stickers, stamps, stamp pad, glue*
- Snap beads*
- Wooden beads*
- Lacing pictures*
- Fine motor puzzle (buttoning, zipping, snapping)*
- Stacking cups/small blocks*
- Echo mike*
- Popsicle sticks*
- Easel*
- Squeeze balls and toys*
- Costumes/dress-up*
- Construction/white paper*
- Tongs*
- Children's scissors #4*
- Geoboard
- Shape Sorting Cube (by Melissa and Doug)
- Snap-Lock Beads (by Fisher Price)
- Latches board (by Melissa and Doug)
- Lace shoe (by Melissa and Doug)
- Work bench
- Play tool box
- **Handy Manny Talkin'** Toolbox
- **Stacking Shapes Pegboard** (by Learning Resources)
  www.sensoryinterventions.com

- **Woodshop Toys Rainbow Numbers** (by Learning Resources) www.sensoryinterventions.com
- **Wooden Pound-A-Peg** (by Melissa and Doug)
- **One, Two, Tie My Shoe** (by Alex)
- **Learn to Lace and Tie Shoe** (by Melissa and Doug)
- **Learn to Dress Jake Doll/ Dressie Bessie/ Dapper Dan**
- **Little Tikes Discover Sounds Drill, Screwdriver, and Hammer**
- **Wooden Cookie Set** (by Melissa and Doug)
- **Wooden Pizza Set** (by Melissa and Doug)
- **Wooden Ice Cream** Set (by Melissa and Doug)
- **Wooden Cake Set** (by Melissa and Doug)
- **Shape, Model, and Mold Dough**
- Rainbow stacker
- Squishy balls
- Wooden cookie set
- Cutting fruit kit
- Ice cream scoop and stack
- **Shape, Model, and Mold Dough**
- **Band in a Box** (10-piece instrument set)
- **Wooden Lacing Beads** (by Melissa and Doug)
- **Lace-A-Puppet:** www.sensoryinterventions.com
- **Magna Doodle**
- **Glow Doodle**
- **Doodle Pro**
- Bristle blocks
- **Bed Bugs** game
- **Operation** game
- **Ants in the Pants** game
- **Mr. Potato Head (by Play School)**
- **Hungry Hungry Hippo (by Play School)**
- **Mega Blocks/ Lego Duplo**
- **Crayola Triangular Markers and Crayons**
- **Crayola Easy Stampers**
- **Crayola Crayon Buddies and First Markers**
- **Wipe Clean/Learn to Write: Numbers, Letters, and Animal Books**

Gross Motor Skill Toys
- Toddler basketball hoop*
- Small basketball*
- Plastic Bowling set*
- Plastic balls (Medium, large)*
- Tunnel*
- Hula hoops (2)*

- Bean bag toss*
- Ring toss*
- Therapy ball*
- Floor balance beam*
- Mini trampoline*
- Kick ball*
- Flashlight*
- Package of small colored plastic balls
- Beach ball
- Colored bean bags
- Horse Shoe Set (by Battat Sports)
- Deluxe Building Blocks Set (Large Cardboard Blocks)
- Toss Across Bean Bag Tic Tac Toe Game (by Mattel)
- Slide (by Little Tykes)

Concept Skill Toys
- Shape sorter clock
- Colored Teddy Bear Counters
- Magnetic calendar
- Weather chart
- Sequence Cards
- Classifying Cards

Self-Care and Activities of Daily Living Toys
- Foam alphabet letters for the tub*
- Count out loud numbers for the tub*
- Plastic tub toys: boats, ducks, planes*
- **Rub-A-Dub** stickers for tub
- **Rub-A-Dub** shaving kit for tub
- Foam shapes
- **Tub Tune** piano, xylophone, drum and flute
- Musical instruments
- Count out loud numbers for tub
- Tubs pots and pans
- Bathtub finger paint and crayons
- **Rub-A-Dub Dunk and Score**
- **Crazy Foam**
- **Sound Spa** (by Homedics)
- **Sound Machine**
- **Wooden Lacing Shoe (**by Melissa and Doug)
- **Basic Skills Board (**garment fasteners by Melissa and Doug)
- **Wooden Cookie Set** (by Melissa and Doug)
- **Wooden Pizza Set** (by Melissa and Doug)

- **Wooden Ice Cream** Set (by Melissa and Doug)
- **Wooden Cake Set** (by Melissa and Doug)

Goody Bag of Toys for Meal Time
- Board books
- Puzzles
- Shape sorter
- Numbers
- Alphabet letters
- Stacking cups
- Beginner pattern blocks (by Melissa and Doug)
- Rainbow stacker
- Hand fidgets
- Flash cards
- Toy keys
- Toy phone,
- Touch and Feel books
- **Magna Doodle**
- Felt story boards
- Squeezums, shakers
- Squishy balls
- Wooden mini puzzles with slide out trays: animals, vehicles, etc.

Goody Bag of Toys for the Car

- Books, plush toys
- Plush toy play sets: fabric house, tool box, Noah's ark, bird house
- Plush toy shape sorter (soft shapes that you put through slots)
- Plush toy catepillar
- **My Little Farm** plush play set (by Gund)
- Squeeze balls: squishy soft balls, sensory balls, bumpy balls
- Finger fidgets
- Toy keys, toy phone,
- **Touch and Feel** books
- Board books
- **Magna Doodle**
- **Doodle Pro**
- **Glow Doodle**
- Felt story boards
- Squeezums, shakers
- Wooden mini puzzles with slide out trays: animals, vehicles, etc.
- View Finder

Appendix II

Websites and Resources

Autism Websites

- www.AutismSpeaks.org

- www.firstsigns.org

- www.autismsocietyofamerica.com

- www.defeatautismnow.org

- www.autismresearchinstitute.com

Websites for Toys and Supplies

- www.melissaanddoug.com

- www.sensoryinterventions.com

- www.Toysrus.com

- www.Toysrus.com/DifferentlyAbled Toy guide for differently-abled kids

- www.achievement-products.com

- www.pfot.com Pocket Full of Therapy Toy Catalog

- www.HABAusa.com

Resources

- *Treating Eating Problems of Children with Autism Spectrum Disorders and Developmental Disabilities* (order from Achievement-Products for Children)

- *Autism Spectrum Disorder: The Complete Guide to Understanding Autism, Asperger's Syndrome, Pervasive Developmental Disorder, and other ASDS* by Chantal Sicile-Kira (Penguin Group Incorporated, 2004)

Appendix III

Early Childhood Intervention

Early Childhood Intervention (ECI) is a state and federally funded government program that provides services for babies and toddlers from birth to three years of age with disabilities or developmental delays. ECI is available in all 50 states; you can locate the ECI office in your city to establish services. In order to obtain their services, it is preferable to have a referral from a pediatrician or hospital, but you can call yourself. Your child does not have to have a diagnosis to receive ECI services. You should contact ECI as soon as you are concerned about your child's development.

After the referral, an ECI service coordinator, occupational therapist, physical therapist, or speech therapist will come to your home to complete an evaluation of your child. A service coordinator (Early Intervention Specialist) works with your family to coordinate all the services necessary to support your child's total development. The Occupational Therapist works with children to become as independent as possible in meaningful life activities as dressing, feeding, toilet training, grooming, social skills, basic play activities, fine motor and visual skills that assist in writing and scissor use, sensory integration skills, function of gross motor skills, and visual perceptual skills needed for reading and writing. The speech therapist helps children learn how to talk; they work on oral motor skills, expressive and receptive language, communication, and articulation. The physical therapist helps children with gross motor body movement, balance, coordination, and strength.

These are highly qualified, trained professionals who will be able to determine if your child qualifies for services; then they will discuss with you what services will be needed. Once your child is determined eligible, you will participate as part of the ECI team in writing up an Individualized Family Service Plan (IFSP). The IFSP describes what services the child will receive, how often, and the cost of services, if applicable.

ECI is successful because it begins at an early age; the earlier the intervention is provided, the better the chance that the child can improve or recover.

Appendix IV

Happy Hearts

How Happy Hearts Was Created

Every morning when Roman was in kindergarten I walked him to his class. One day before I said goodbye he said, "Mom, is your heart happy? You have to have a happy heart." He proceeded to take his hands and made them into a heart shape and said, "Happy Hearts, Mom!" I in turn made a happy heart sign with my hands and said, "My heart is very happy and Happy Hearts to you, too." And that's how "Happy Hearts" began. From that day on he would say, "Have a happy hearts day," and would make a happy heart.

Every morning before school began I read to the entire kindergarten class, a total of 120 children, and at the end of reading time I taught them all how to make the "Happy Hearts" sign with their hands. So each day, I ended reading time by saying, "A great big smile makes happy hearts;" and they all made the Happy Hearts sign with their hands and we sang the song below (to the tune of "Bad Day" by Alvin and the Chipmunks).

At our book signings for *Raindrops on Roman*, Roman drew a happy heart on every book that he signed because he wants everyone's heart to be happy. It became his "logo" and people wanted their books signed with a happy heart.

So to all of you, have a Happy Hearts day, from our happy hearts to yours.

© 2009 by Roman Scott

(Make up hand gestures for each line)

"I'll have a great day.
I'll do well in school.
I'll play with my friends,
And I'll follow the rules,
I'll have a great day.
Have a Happy Hearts day!"

Appendix V

I Will Always Love You

Sweet child,
I will always love you;
I will never leave you nor forsake you.
What joy you give me;
what courage you show me.
I respect your determination
and fight to get better.
Though my heart breaks
for your struggle and what we go through,
your condition and limitations
only augment my love for you.
For I love you enough
to stand the things I must do.
No matter what you need from me,
I will be there for you.
Anything that you can give,
that's all I'll ask of you.
Your love and strength inspire me;
I will be there for you.

~ Elizabeth Burton Scott, M.A.

Appendix VI

Dare To Care

Dear Parents, Teachers, and Therapists:

It is our goal that all students in schools everywhere learn to Dare to Care for those who are differently-abled. We need to teach all children to accept and be friends with children with autism, or any child with a disability. Parents of children with autism and children with autism often feel isolated and lonely because people may not know how to react around them, or may react negatively to their behaviors. It is hard enough dealing with the problems that are associated with autism, but all the more difficult when their peers are not accepting of them.

Many children with autism display odd behaviors or "quirks," such as repetitive actions, or may be difficult to converse with; but we as the adults must accept these behaviors and teach our children how to reach out and interact with them in a very positive and loving manner.

We should break this cycle of turning away and Dare to Care for every child with autism and every differently-abled child. Let us honor the differences and accept what each child can do. Listen to what they have to say, engage in their interests and help them with their challenges, whether social, behavioral, or physical, and respect them for who they are.

Do not be afraid or embarrassed if they do something that may seem odd or different, just be a friend and care for them. Appreciate their kindness, celebrate their abilities, and the fact that they are trying to be the best they can be. To make a friend, you have to be a friend.

Sincerely,

Elizabeth Scott and Lynne Gillis

ABOUT THE AUTHORS

Elizabeth Burton Scott, M.A. is a graduate of Northwestern University in Evanston, Illinois. She has a Master's Degree in Elementary Education, and taught second and third grades for seven years. With her professional skills and her deep devotion as a mother, she persevered in leading her son Roman through his early childhood years to recover from 45 symptoms of autism. She has published her story—a true love story—about their journey in her book title, *Raindrops on Roman: Overcoming Autism: A Message of Hope*. Her mission now is to serve as a coach, consultant, and speaker for professionals and families helping children with autism. She lives in Dallas, Texas with her husband and son.

Visit www.autismprayer.com where you can download for FREE any one or all three prayers (suitable for framing) that Elizabeth wrote:

- *A Mother's Autism Prayer*

- *A Prayer for the Parent of a Child with Autism*

- *I Will Always Love You*

Lynne Gillis received her B.S. degree in Occupational Therapy from Columbia University, College of Physicians and Surgeons, School of Occupational Therapy in 1971. She is a member of the American Occupational Therapy Association. In her 30 years in the field of occupational therapy she specialized in pediatric occupational therapy working in private and public schools, rehabilitation outpatient clinics, early intervention programs, and home-based therapy programs. Lynne was an initial advocate of early intervention programs, classroom treatment groups and the consultative model. Her professional experiences and enthusiasm for the profession have made her a role model for occupational therapists working with children. She lives in Mattapoisett, Massachusetts with her husband, children and grandchildren.

Robert D. Reed Publishers Order Form

Call in your order for fast service and quantity discounts
(541) 347- 9882

OR *order on-line at* **www.rdrpublishers.com** *using PayPal.*

OR *order by mail: Make a copy of this form; enclose payment information:*

Robert D. Reed Publishers, 1380 Face Rock Drive, Bandon, OR 97411

Send indicated books to:

Name _____ Address _____

City _____ State ____ Zip _____ Phone _____

Fax _____ Cell _____ E-Mail _____

Payment by check ☐ or credit card ☐ *(All major credit cards are accepted.)*

Name on card _____ Card Number _____

Exp. Date _____ Last 3-Digit number on back of card _____

TO BE A BETTER PARENT OR PROFESSIONAL WORKING WITH CHILDREN

Autism Recovery Manual of Skills and Drills   *Qty.*
by Elizabeth Scott, M.A.& Lynne Gillis ....$16.95 _____

Raindrops on Roman: Overcoming Autism: A Message of Hope
by Elizabeth Scott ....$14.95 _____

Special Foods for Special Kids by Todd Adelman and Jodi Behrend ....$16.95 _____

Remembering Pets by Gina Dalpra-Berman ....$14.95 _____

Violet's Vision by Fran Fisher ....$12.95 _____

Tyrone: a Turtle Tale by Sue Foley ....$14.95 _____

California Squisine by Malcolm Kushner ....$11.95 _____

The Legend of Baeoh: How Baeoh Got His Stripes by Lucas Taekwon Lee ..... $17.95 _____

101 Ways to be a Long-Distance Super Dad… and Mom too!
By George Newman ....$ 9.95 _____

Rocky the Lighthouse Makes a Difference by Jeffrey Noel ....$14.95 _____

The Biggest and Brightest Light by Marilyn Perlyn ....$16.95 _____

ADD: The 20-Hour Solution
by Mark Steinberg, Ph.D. and Siegfried Othmer, Ph.D. ....$14.95 _____

A Kid's Herb Book by Lesley Tierra, L.Ac., AHG ....$19.95 _____

Unleashing Kids' Potential by Karen A. Waldron, Ph.D ....$11.95 _____

Total Number of Books _____ Total Amount _____

Note: Shipping is $3.50 1st book + $1 for each additional book.   Shipping _____

THE TOTAL _____